Cambridge Elements ☰

Elements in Beckett Studies
edited by
Dirk Van Hulle
University of Oxford
Mark Nixon
University of Reading

ABSORPTION AND THEATRICALITY

On Ghost Trio

Conor Carville
University of Reading

CAMBRIDGE
UNIVERSITY PRESS

CAMBRIDGE
UNIVERSITY PRESS

University Printing House, Cambridge CB2 8BS, United Kingdom

One Liberty Plaza, 20th Floor, New York, NY 10006, USA

477 Williamstown Road, Port Melbourne, VIC 3207, Australia

314–321, 3rd Floor, Plot 3, Splendor Forum, Jasola District Centre,
New Delhi – 110025, India

103 Penang Road, #05–06/07, Visioncrest Commercial, Singapore 238467

Cambridge University Press is part of the University of Cambridge.

It furthers the University's mission by disseminating knowledge in the pursuit of
education, learning, and research at the highest international levels of excellence.

www.cambridge.org
Information on this title: www.cambridge.org/9781009001175
DOI: 10.1017/9781009000369

First published 2022

A catalogue record for this publication is available from the British Library.

ISBN 978-1-009-00117-5 Paperback
ISSN 2632-0746 (online)
ISSN 2632-0738 (print)

Absorption and Theatricality

On *Ghost Trio*

Elements in Beckett Studies

DOI: 10.1017/9781009000369
First published online: February 2022

Conor Carville
University of Reading

Author for correspondence: Conor Carville, c.carville@reading.ac.uk

Abstract: Samuel Beckett's 1976 television play *Ghost Trio* is one of his most beautiful and mysterious works. It is also the play that most clearly demonstrates Beckett's imaginative and aesthetic engagement with the visual arts and the history of painting in particular. Drawing on the work of Stanley Cavell and Michael Fried, *On Ghost Trio* demonstrates Beckett's exploration of the relationship between theatricality, absorption and objecthood, and shows how his work anticipates the development of video and installation art. In doing so, Conor Carville develops a new and highly original reading of Beckett's art, rooted in both archival sources and philosophical aesthetics.

Keywords: Beckett, aesthetics, art, Cavell, Fried

ISBNs: 9781009001175 (PB), 9781009000369 (OC)
ISSNs: 2632-0746 (online), 2632-0738 (print)

Contents

1 Introduction

Beckett's TV play *Ghost Trio* was at first titled *Tryst* (Beckett, 1976b). The word, meaning an assignation, was originally used in the context of hunting, to mean a fixed meeting point in the woods. Yet there are other etymological lineages that are worth pointing to as a context for the approach to be taken in this Element. The *OED* connects tryst with the middle English and Scottish 'trist(e)', meaning confidence, expectation and hope. This is in turn linked to the familiar modern noun *trust*: 'Firm belief in the reliability, truth, or ability of someone or something; confidence or faith in a person or thing, or in an attribute of a person or thing'. Scepticism, philosophical doubt and the problem of other minds might be seen as the opposites of such a firm belief or trust, and scepticism together with the question of aesthetic autonomy will guide my reading of *Ghost Trio*.

In the published script of the play a lone figure, F, sits in a stark room, listening intently to Beethoven's Fifth Piano Trio on a cassette recorder (Beckett, 1990, 405–14). He responds to an apparent noise at the door, opens and closes it, then makes a circuit of the room, opening and closing its window, looking at the bed and mirror, then returning to the chair and cassette to again immerse himself in the music. This is all then twice repeated. On the first two occasions the camera is, for the most part, at a distance from him, and his actions seem to be directed by V, an off-screen voice who has already introduced the world of the play, and named the contents of the room, in the early moments of the piece. During the third circuit the camera is much closer to F, V is silent, the music more prominent, and we are on several occasions allowed to see from F's point of view. The play was written in 1975, and first shown on the BBC in 1977 as part of the portmanteau broadcast *Shades*, alongside ' . . . but the clouds . . . ' and *Not I*. A second and slightly different version, *Geistertrio*, appeared on Süddeutscher Rundfunk in the same year. In this Element I will examine the BBC version, as it is closer to the published text.

In one strand of what follows I am going to argue for a reading of the play as an examination of trust or belief, the kind of trust that must necessarily accompany or attend the hope or possibility of a tryst. One of the ways in which *Ghost Trio* asks for this trust is through its difficulty. The play puts the very idea of drama, and TV drama, under considerable stress. It tests the limits of the conventions that make a twenty-minute combination of language, sound and image recognizable as theatre. At times, it seems that what we are watching is not a finished play at all, but an experiment in behavioural psychology, or a rehearsal. As Beckett dismantles our assumptions about character, performance and intention, the audience must overcome their scepticism and keep faith with the idea that an aesthetic experience persists, that what they are watching is still drama.

Stanley Cavell's understanding of 'acknowledgement' as an essential component of the armoury of modernist painting will be useful here, in that the term forms a bridge in Cavell's aesthetic thought between scepticism, the beholder's judgement and what he calls the automatism of the artwork. Cavell:

> Any painting might teach you what is true of all painting. A modernist painting teaches you this *by* acknowledgment – which means that responding to it must itself have the form of accepting it as a painting, or rejecting it. In ordinary cases of acknowledging something, I can acknowledge only what I know to be true *of me*, whereas this painting is supposed to be speaking for all painting, painting as such. (Cavell, 1979b, 109–10)

There is a patently Kantian concern in Cavell's stance here, an attention to the possibility of translating subjective aesthetic assessment to the realm of the objective. Importantly, however, Cavell replaces the Kantian judgement of beauty with the notion of acknowledgement of the status of the painting *as a painting*. Shortly after, Cavell emphasizes the necessarily autonomous nature of the artwork, and draws on Beckett's theatre in order to do so:

> The quality I have in mind [i.e. autonomy] might be expressed as openness achieved through *instantaneousness* – which is a way of characterizing the *candid*. The candid has a reverse feature as well: that it must occur independently of me or any audience, that it must be complete without me, in that sense *closed* to me. This is why candidness in acting was achieved by the actor's complete concentration within the character, absolutely denying any control of my awareness upon him. When theatrical conventions lost their naturalness and became matters of mutual complicity between actor and audience, then serious drama had to deny my control openly – by removing, say, any 'character' for the actor to disappear into (Beckett), or by explicitly wedging the mutual consciousness of actor and audience between the actor and his character (Brecht). (Cavell, 1979b, 111)

We will soon be returning to Cavell's account of Beckett's drama in much more detail. But it is useful to introduce early on this complex of candidness, character, autonomy and audience, as these are some of the key dramatic conventions that Beckett chooses to examine in *Ghost Trio*.

The duality of openness and closedness cited above is a compact central to the thinking of Cavell's friend and interlocutor the art historian and critic Michael Fried, who like Cavell sees the self-sufficiency and integrity of a painting's world as dependent on the way it ignores, excludes or otherwise discounts the person looking at it (Fried, 1988). In Fried's art-historical work on eighteenth-century painting, this plays out as a dialectic between the 'closed' depiction of figures who are, like Cavell's actors, intensely caught up, engrossed in some thought, attitude or activity, and the way this absorption, as Fried terms it, 'opens' the picture to disinterested aesthetic contemplation. A painting or sculpture that does not do this, that actively addresses or solicits the viewer by, for example, having a figure gesture out to them, or by overtly placing the beholder in a position of what Cavell calls control, through manipulation of form or perspective, is what Fried castigates as 'theatrical'.

Beckett too had concerns with a mode of painting constructed to directly address a beholder. This is apparent from his complaints about the landscape painting in the London National Gallery in a letter of late 1934. Here 'Landscape [is] "promoted" to the emotions of the hiker, promoted as concerned with the hiker', he writes, then cites Ruisdael's *Entrance to the Forest*, with its foreground pathway inviting the beholder's access, arguing that the painting fails to grasp that 'there is no forest any more nor any commerce with the forest, its dimensions are its secret, it has no communications to make' (Beckett, 2009, 222). By contrast with such tactics, Beckett very often praised pictures that exhibited closed or absorptive traits. Remaining with the Dutch genre painting he loved, one example is the little man in Hans Moloenar's *The Smoker* (Beckett, 1936–7, 5.1.37). There are many others (Carville, 2018, 124–5).

Ghost Trio also turns on images of absorption. The clearest example of this is the degree of F's immersion in the music as he sits, crouched over his cassette recorder. The unavoidable implication is that he is intensely moved by the music he hears, and the way in which the music is often withheld from the audience only adds to the suggestion of a sensibility that is cut off from us, yet experiencing profound affect. Other moments too seem designed to raise the question of what exactly F is thinking or imagining, as he gazes raptly at the pallet, for example, or examines his own face in the mirror.

This network of ideas – absorption or candidness, the relationship between character and actor, the questions of theatricality or control – offers a valuable means for assessing one of Beckett's hints about *Ghost Trio*. As James Knowlson has pointed out, the playwright suggested that Ronald Pickup read Kleist's 'On the Puppet Theatre' as part of his preparation for the role of F (Knowlson and Pilling, 1979, 279). Kleist's story turns on the strange elegance of the puppets of the title, which the narrator implies is a function of their absolute lack of self-consciousness, a point that he goes on to gloss through the story of the dancing bear, another example of the way in which for Kleist selflessness, the lack of self-consciousness, issues in an absolute, unearthly grace of movement.

There could perhaps be no more apt illustration of Michael Fried's ideal of absorption. Indeed, in his book *Why Photography Matters as Art as Never*

Before, Fried describes Kleist's essay as 'one of the master theoretical texts in the anti-theatrical tradition' (Fried, 2008, 245–6; Kleist, 1982). For both Fried and Kleist, the depiction of an impenetrable figure, one that resists any access to its interiority, whether because in Kleist's case the puppet or bear does not possess such inwardness or, in Fried's analysis of paintings like Chardin's *Soap Bubbles* (Figure 1), because the figure is so bound up in action or reflection that the beholder registers his or her own exclusion from the scene, this impenetrability carries with it the serene autonomy of art. For Fried, as for Kleist (and, I will argue, for Beckett), character – the character of the bear or the puppet – stand in for the self-containment and independence of the artefact. As we have seen, in Cavell's terms this is the *candid*, that which is 'closed to me' as an audience member, achieved by 'the actor's complete concentration within the character, absolutely denying any control of my awareness upon him' (Cavell, 1979b, 111).

And yet, as we have also noted, Cavell regards Beckett's work as distanced from this mode. Candidness or absorption is not present, cannot be present, in Beckett's theatre, because there is no character into which the actor can withdraw. There is a point of contact here with Fried's account of French painting later than Chardin or Greuze, and the fate of absorption in modernity. For, in *Manet's Modernism*, Fried argues that the tactics of artists like Chardin were no longer available as a means of combatting theatricality (Fried, 1999). By the

Figure 1 Chardin, *Soap Bubbles*, Metropolitan Museum, New York

1860s, the absorbed characters that appeared in certain French paintings had come to seem thin and artificial, in the same way that Cavell sees candidness becoming impossible to take seriously in the theatre. Hence Manet's decision to purloin and repurpose theatricality itself, in great canvases like *Le Déjeuner sur l'herbe* or *The Old Musician*. In such pictures the central figure addresses the viewer directly, but does not cede control to them. Rather than confirming the beholder's point of view by offering their gaze, they challenge and wrong-foot. Instead of disappearing into a character, they affirm their own presence shamelessly. In a painting like *Olympia*, for example, the model does not vanish into the mythic character, but is displayed, candidly, as a model, and this was one of the reasons that the painting attracted such opprobrium.

2 Modernism, Painting, Tragedy

Where modernist painting exposes the model, we might be tempted to say, modernist theatre reveals the actor, exposing the mechanics of performance and breaching the fourth wall. But this does not do justice to the subtlety of Manet's procedure. As Fried points out, the boredom and vacancy of the experience of sitting for a portrait are present in the gaze of Manet's women (Fried, 1999, 399).[1] It is not as if Manet unmasks the sleight-of-hand of allegorical painting and depicts instead an authentic individual of his own time. Rather, what is left is more like a pure, empty pose, a blank unnerving gaze. Cavell's distinction between Brecht and Beckett makes a similar distinction between two versions of modernist theatre. To say, with Cavell, that in Brecht the complicity between actor and audience intervenes between actor and character suggests the routines of defamiliarization that the German writer deploys: caricature, shifts in genre, song, placards, etc. The actors are self-consciously part of this assemblage, pulling their own strings to mug and wink at the spectator. The two elements of actor and role are constantly in play, and the audience sees this. This is the now-standard practice of modernist self-reflexivity, seen also in Pirandello and others. In his essay devoted to Beckett's *Endgame*, however, Cavell suggests that this kind of complicity with the audience should not be foisted onto Beckett's work:

> Brecht calls for new relations between an actor and his role, and between the actor and his audience: theater is to defeat theater. But in Beckett there is no role towards which the actor can maintain intelligence, and he has nothing more to tell his audience than his characters' words convey.
>
> (Cavell, 1976a, 160)

---

[1] Fried describes Manet's faces in terms that would have appealed to Beckett: 'frozen or immobilized – we might say petrified' (Fried, 1999, 340).

Instead of the actor moving in and out of character, or holding character at a distance through irony, in Beckett the actor has no recourse to character at all. For Cavell this means that in Beckett *acting itself disappears*:

> The figures up there are not acting, but undergoing something which is taking its course, they are not characters. And we could also say: the words are not spoken by them, to one another; they are occurring to them. It is a play performed not by actors, but by sufferers, clowns.
>
> (Cavell, 1976a, 159)

One way to draw out what Cavell means here is through a short thought experiment. Think of a piece in which the actors wear concealed earpieces, through which their lines are dictated. The actors have not been told anything about the characters they will play. They do not learn their lines, and thus do not, cannot, anticipate the words they will deliver. They are in the moment *with* the words. In this sense they are not acting, and are not characters. They are not inhabiting their roles, as they do not know what the roles are. They are passive, undergoing events rather than initiating them: they suffer rather than act. Cavell insists that a similar quality of what he calls 'continuous presentness' is intrinsic to Beckett's work (Cavell, 1976b, 322). It is present too in Acts I and II of *Ghost Trio*, although the audience can hear the words that, in our thought experiment, are not audible.

Cavell also finds continuous presentness in classical tragedy. Or perhaps more accurately, he finds it in the ideal reception of tragedy, when the audience is completely immersed in the time of the play, having given up their own present in favour of the present of the actors as it happens or occurs to them onstage. In such moments, as Cavell puts it, every detail can, potentially at least, be significant, and the concentration in the present destroys both memory and desire, recollection and anticipation, on the part, it seems, of both actors and audience (Cavell, 1976b, 313–4). Cavell finds another example of such acting in Paul Scofield's performance as the king in Peter Brook's *Lear* (a notoriously Beckettian production):

> One wants to say not that the character we know is embodied for us, but that the performance is about embodiment. It displays not merely the end-points of thought and impulse, but the drama by which impulse and thought find (and lose) their way through the body. (Cavell, 1976a, 159)

We remember here Manet's painting of the pose rather than the character, the way his pictures counter the theatrical by excavating new, ironic forms of absorption, such as the bored prostitute blankly staring as she lies on the divan. Scofield's Lear is of a different order, but the notion of a thought lost in the body (rather than explicitly expressed by it) is certainly anti-theatrical in Fried's sense.

Cavell refines his description further by saying that 'it is not merely that the words are so perfectly motivated that they appear to be occurring to the character, but that the style or delivery is itself one of occurring' (Cavell, 1976a, 159). This is an inflection of his earlier description of Hamm and Clov: 'They are not characters. And we could also say: the words are not spoken by them, to one another; they are occurring to them.' If the words are not spoken, neither are they addressed, as Cavell makes clear, and again we can see how this mode of acting, whether encouraged by Beckett or discovered in *Lear* by Scofield and Brook, is anti-theatrical. It trades on the legacy of an absorption that is not now possible in the way it once was. The immersive quality of classical absorption or candidness is replaced by a kind of evacuation: the presence of the actor or image is heightened through a lack of the standard cues of interiority, so that attention is displaced onto the sheer fact of embodiment. As Cavell puts it elsewhere, in such work 'the presentness achieved by certainty of the senses cannot compensate for the presentness which had been elaborated through our old absorption in the world' (Cavell, 1976b, 323). That is to say, empirical verification through the audience's perception, without their absorptive immersion in the performance, produces a strange, new form of experience. This is an especially suggestive point, given the way, as we shall see, Act I of *Ghost Trio* sharply juxtaposes empirical knowledge and failed absorption. We will be returning in detail to Cavell's concerns about knowledge and acknowledgement; suffice it to say here that he sees the drama's ability to induce a mode of consciousness that attends exclusively to the present moment as being a means of suspending the kinds of knowledge he associates with certain forms of Enlightenment rationalism. In such circumstances it is the trust in art's autonomy that belies scepticism.

These lines on 'presentness' come from a later essay devoted entirely to *King Lear*, which can also aid an understanding of Cavell's Beckett. 'The Avoidance of Love' sets out a detailed account of tragedy, and although *Endgame* is only mentioned once, Beckett's play is a constant presence, for Cavell spends much time exploring the fate of tragedy in contemporary life and art, and clearly has his earlier essay in mind. Once again, the question of audience is paramount. In classical tragedy the audience, although it is ignored by the actors, and so cannot be said to be in their *presence*, transposes itself into the *present* of the actors and the play. This making-present constitutes the acknowledgement, by the audience, of the play as play, as well as their trust of the characters as independent individuals who act and suffer.

> We are not in, and cannot put ourselves in, the presence of the characters; but we are in, or can put ourselves in, their *present*. It is in making their present ours, their moments as they occur, that we complete our acknowledgement of

them. But this requires making their present *theirs*. And that requires us to face not only the porousness of our knowledge (of, for example the motives of their actions and the consequences they care about) but the repudiation of our perception altogether. (Cavell, 1976b, 337)

We should note the phrase 'their moments as they occur' here: it is this release of the event into the strange temporality of what Cavell calls 'occurrence' that seems to licence the beholder/audience's necessary 'repudiation of perception'. This reference to the mechanics of perception is also vitally important, signalling the way Cavell is pitching the mode of attention being explored here against the empirical order he associates with knowledge and scepticism. When we are wholly given over to the play, having sacrificed our own present and perception, it is in this absolute vulnerability that we are able to witness and understand, to acknowledge, 'the fact and true cause' of the suffering of the other. We are not told by Cavell *how* such insights are effected, though there are hints that it is an intuitive, pre-reflective, non-rational process. The closest he comes to specifying in what his notion of absorption consists comes through a parallel with the music of Beethoven, another intriguing parallel with *Ghost Trio*, given the role of music in the play. In this music:

> the quality we are to perceive is one of directed motion, controlled by relations of keys, by rate of alteration, and by length and articulation of phrases. We do not know where this motion can stop and *we do not understand why it has begun here, so we do not know where we stand nor why we are there.* The drama consists in following this out and in finding out what it takes to follow this out. The specific comparison with Shakespeare's drama has to do with the two most obvious facts about what is required in following this music: first, that one hears its directedness; second, that one hears *only what is happening now.* (Cavell, 1976b, 321)

Here we have another possible avenue into the nature of dramatic time as 'occurrence' or, as Cavell puts it, here and in the *Endgame* essay, as 'happening'. The term suggests a kind of accentuated indeterminacy and unpredictability, which seems in the case of Beckett's drama to be aided by the 'characterless' mode of acting the script elicits, and which an actor like Scofield and a director like Brook can also find in Shakespeare. The condition of not knowing beginning nor end, nor where we are, nor why, is the condition of happening. Notably it is also the condition of the actors in *Endgame* as Cavell sees it. And as he makes clear, in Beckett's work the condition of the actors is also the condition of the audience: 'no one in the place, on the stage or in the house, knows better than anyone else what is happening, no one has a better right to speak than anyone else' (Cavell, 1976a, 158). In other words, it is this relationship to pure immediate happening, to continuous presentness, that breaches the fourth wall, and in so doing abolishes the audience as usually conceived and with that theatricality – the direct appeal to the audience – in Fried's sense.

3 'Good Evening'

The *Lear* essay is enlightening in the way it contrasts tragic acknowledgement of the suffering of others with the alternative modes of knowledge available in the contemporary cultural, technical and political context. Here, Cavell argues, the proliferation of the news media makes events available to us, all the time, and we to them. We thus experience 'everything happening as overwhelmingly present, like events in old theatre' (Cavell, 1976b, 347). Yet there is also a difference: 'a tragedy is about a particular death', whereas 'now [that] we are surrounded by inexplicable pain and death, no death is more mysterious or portentous than the others' (Cavell, 1976b, 344). As a result, we no longer know what is and is not news . . . what is and is not relevant to one's life.

It is this indiscriminate quality of the rolling news that creates issues for the reception of tragedy: which of the daily deaths, the daily tragedies, should I respond to, make myself present to? For I am present to them all, and this is what Cavell explicitly calls, after Fried, the theatrical quality of the world today (Cavell, 1976b, 344). All of these events are addressed to me, as a beholder. That is to say, I am assumed to be an actor in what is happening: I am not ignored, as an audience should be. And it is true, even now, that the presiding form of the news media is the direct apostrophe to the viewer ('Good evening', as V says in the first line of *Ghost Trio*). We are presented to what happens, willy-nilly. As a result, Cavell points out:

> Because we are [. . .] actors in what is happening, nothing can be present to us to which we are not present. Of course we can still know, more than ever, what is going on. What we do not now know is what there is to acknowledge, what it is I am to make present, what I am to make myself present to.
>
> (Cavell, 1976b, 346)

This has consequences in turn for what we might think of as the ethical comportment towards the image.

> I know there is inexplicable pain and death everywhere, and now if I ask myself why I do nothing the answer must be, I choose not to. That is, doing nothing is no longer something which has a place insured by ceremony; it is the thing I am doing. (Cavell, 1976b, 346)

Theatricality, in the pejorative sense that Cavell shares with Fried, has invaded the world, has left its ceremonial surroundings and is all-pervasive, so that the salutary 'silence, hiddenness and withdrawal' that, in the context of the classical tragic drama, gave us respite from scepticism and from our failures of acknowledgement, and allowed us to flex our possibilities of empathy, is now ubiquitous, but functions differently. Our silence in front of the television screen means, simply, isolation and individual captivation rather than communal awe. And it is such incapacitating awe that is the condition of true recognition of the pain of others. In the theatre, helplessness to intervene is also the *freedom* to judge ethically. As Cavell puts it of classical tragedy:

> Their fate, up there, out there, is that they must act, they are in the arena in which action is ineluctable. My *freedom* is that I am not now in the arena. Everything which can be done is being done. The present in which action is alone possible is fully occupied. It is not that my space is different from theirs but that I have no space within which I can move. It is not that my time is different from theirs but that I have no present apart from theirs.
>
> (Cavell, 1976b, 338–9)

In this last quotation one can see the Kantian foundations on which Cavell is building. For Kant the ethical is noumenal, free from the bonds of time and space, and thus undetermined. For Cavell, it seems that the conventions of the theatre, its ritual practices and communal agreements, institute a dichotomy between stage and audience. He outlines the opposition earlier in the *Lear* essay, writing, 'Kant tells us that man lives in two worlds, in one of which he is free and in the other determined. *It is as if in a theater these two worlds are faced off against one another*' (Cavell, 1976b, 317; my emphasis). Ethical freedom and aesthetic disinterest thus reinforce each other, and in the breaking of this compact both fail simultaneously. To repeat, in the theatre, doing nothing is freedom. It comes, for Cavell, of the audience's self-effacement, their awe-struck ceding of their own time and space to that of the play. Outside the theatre, however, it is nihilism, the dumb fascination with the spectacle. As Cavell puts it, on the news everything is offered as relevant, but tragedy, by contrast, 'requires that we reveal ourselves and [. . .] this *is not occasioned by showing me that something happening is relevant to me* – that is inescapably the case – but by showing me something to which I am relevant, or irrelevant' (Cavell, 1976b, 349; my emphasis).[2] The last point again stresses the relationship between this ethical comportment towards pressing events and aesthetic disinterest, and takes us back to anti-theatricality. Disinterest, one might say, is the exclusion of involuntary relevance, the framing of a happening as something to which I must *make* myself relevant, rather than be captivated by.

---

[2] The artwork's ability to stage this duality is reinscribed at another level in the modernist painting's demand that beholder must judge whether to 'accept it or reject it as a painting'. See Cavell, 1979b, 109–10, quoted earlier.

These reflections on relevance, helplessness, awe, and so on are all from the essay on *Lear*. But the earlier essay on Beckett also suggests that *Endgame* departs from previous drama through its operations on the concept of audience. As Cavell writes there:

> The aesthetic problem about Beckett's dramaturgy [...] concerns how the people comprising the audience are different from those same people when they are not an audience. Partially the answer has to do with the conventions of the theater: getting rid of the audience is not necessarily a matter of emptying the theater, but of removing the concept and the status of audience.
> (Cavell, 1976a, 157)

Hence when, in the essay on *King Lear*, Cavell considers tragedy 'could it now be written', it is not surprising that he focusses on the question of the audience and its separateness from the actors on stage:

> The point of my presence at these events is to join in confirming this separateness. Confirming it as neither a blessing nor a curse, but a fact, the fact of having one life – not one rather than two, but this one rather than any other. *I cannot confirm it alone*. Rather, it is the nature of this tragedy that its actors have to confirm their separateness alone, through isolation, the denial of others. What is purged is my difference from others, in everything but separateness. (Cavell, 1976b, 338; my italics)

It would seem that *Endgame*'s innovation turns on this sense of 'joining', the communal aspect of theatre-going. In Shakespeare the actors confirm their separateness alone, through denying the audience, while the audience confirm their own separateness from the actors as a group, as an audience. As Cavell restates it: 'to empty ourselves of all other difference can be confirmed in the presence of an audience, of the community, because every difference established between us [...] is established by the community'.

It is the latter aspect that has now changed for Cavell, and this new state of affairs is specifically charged to the atomization of audience, which is linked to the collapse of universalizing aesthetic judgement of the Kantian type:

> Tragedy, could it now be written, would not show us that we are helpless – it never did, and we are not. It would show us, what it always did, *why we (as audience)* are helpless. Classically, the reason was that pain and death were in our presence when we were not in theirs. Now the reason is that we absent ourselves from them. Earlier, the members of the audience revealed only their common difference from the actors. Now each man is revealed privately, for there is no audience, apart from each man's making himself an audience; what is revealed is that there is no community, no identity of condition, but that each man has his reasons, good or bad, for choosing not to act. After a tragedy now, should one be written, the members of the audience would not

> see one another measured against nature again, but ranged against it, as if
> nature has been wiped out and the circle of social and historical arbitrariness
> is now complete. (Cavell, 1976b, 346)

Again, this is from the *Lear* essay. But when Cavell writes that 'nature has been
wiped out', we are reminded both of Kant's judgement of teleology, where the
purposefulness of nature serves as ground, and Clov's 'There's no more nature'.
Cavell draws a parallel between absenting oneself from the labour of universalizing aesthetic judgement, the alienation from nature as purposeful order and
the collapse of community into individualism.

Today tragedy examines why, *as audience* as Cavell carefully puts it, we
are unable to make the scene of pain and death present, to bring it into our
own presence by assuming its presentness, its immediacy, in the way the
audience of classic tragedy was able to. Instead, we make ourselves absent,
as audience or community, and relate solely as individuals. Again, here we
can see how *Endgame* carries out a variation on this operation, according to
Cavell's earlier work on Beckett. The terms are similar to the plight of the
audience in the era of mass media, but in Beckett's hands the result is
genuinely tragic. The difference seems to turn on the question of relevance,
which is in turn a question of address. The news addresses one directly and
makes everything relevant. In Beckett, by contrast, address of any sort
vanishes. We must, as individuals, and in the absence of an ordered nature
or communal norms, assess the relevance of what we see. For both Cavell and
Fried this is the *sine qua non* of the modernist artwork. Thus the question of
relevance or irrelevance, and the acceptance or rejection of the artwork, are
coterminous.

Crucially, the innovation that allows Beckett to suspend address is the
erasure of character. Not only do his characters fail to address each other,
they address no one, or God alone. In effect, Beckett both absolutizes and
abolishes the boundary between audience and actor. If each audience member
is an individual audience, an audience of one, then the relations between each
theatre-goer, and between each of these and the stage, is the same. As is the
rapport, or lack of it, between actor and actor. The boundary between stage and
audience ramifies throughout the house, falling now between actor and actor,
spectator and actor, spectator and spectator. All are the same, and all are
different. As Cavell puts it of Beckett's production: 'no one in the place, on
the stage or in the house, knows better than anyone else what is happening, no
one has a better right to speak than anyone else'. In this combination of
atomization and impersonality, 'theater becomes the brute metaphysical fact
of separateness' (Cavell, 1976a, 160).

4 The Fact of Separateness: Beckett and Scepticism

Cavell's phrase catches one of Beckett's early and lasting intuitions: a deep scepticism that is often worked out through the analysis of painting. This scepticism reflects what Beckett called the 'ultimate hard irreducible inorganic singleness' of each human being (Beckett, 2009, 536). Cavell's formulation in his reading of *Endgame* has the considerable merit of enabling the translation of such an ontology into considerations of aesthetic form. For Cavell, Beckett's attitude towards audience does not simply 'break the fourth wall' and so abolish the audience by addressing them directly (although he does do this, as Cavell admits). Much more strikingly, and less familiar in conventional accounts of modernism and after, Beckett dissolves audience by in effect absolutizing the fourth wall, removing even the most minimal conventions of address that make acting interpretable. In this way he is making of his drama a mode of 'separation' akin to that obtaining between people, or 'minds'. One corollary of this is that the relation between an individual audience member, and the happenings and occurrences onstage, is a transposition of that between individuals, rather than one between a community working with its own set of approved generic conventions for the encounter with art, and the artefact itself.

Beckett sees exactly the same structure in Jack B. Yeats' pictures:

> The way he puts down a man's head & a woman's head side by side, or face to face, is terrifying, two irreducible singlenesses & the impassable immensity between. I suppose that is what gives the stillness to his pictures, as though the convention were suddenly suspended, the convention & performance of love & hate, joy & pain, giving & being given, taking & being taken. A kind of petrified insight into one's ultimate hard irreducible inorganic singleness being. (Beckett, 2009, 536)

Or again, writing to Thomas MacGreevy:

> Do you remember the picture of a man sitting under a fuchsia hedge, reading, with his back turned to the sea & the thunder clouds? One does not realize how still his pictures are till one looks at others, almost petrified, a sudden suspension of the performance, of the convention of sympathy & antipathy, meeting & parting, joy & sorrow being. (Beckett, 2009, 540)

This brings us back to the question of absorption, and the very possibility of its depiction in modernity. In the last quotation, Beckett is referring to Yeats' *The Storm*, one of the many anti-theatrical paintings that he admired and appealed to in moments that anticipate his own mature aesthetic. The lone figure reading by the sea is reminiscent of innumerable naively absorptive antecedents. But Yeats' modernism demands something more than this. And yet, rather than following Manet's solution of direct address to the beholder, the absorbed figure of *The Storm* is not only clearly immersed in the book he holds, his body appears to be leaching into the landscape around him.[3] Conversely, where anti-theatrical contemporaries such as Hammershoi relied on the familiar absorptive effects produced by stark, single outlines, framed interiors and bold chiaroscuro to generate a sense of concentrated self-containment, Yeats has his figure's intensity seemingly saturate the whole canvas. As a result, the picture 'keeps all significance continuously before our senses' (Cavell, 1976b, 313). The latter is Cavell's description of Shakespeare's achievement in 'Avoiding Love', describing *King Lear*, and later in the same essay Cavell expands on it slightly, saying such a tactic 'demands a continuous attention to what is happening at each here and now, as if everything of significance is happening at this moment'. These short accounts of the mode of attention prescribed by *King Lear* are apt also to describe Yeats' anti-theatricality. Both *Lear* and *The Storm*, despite their differing media, achieve what Cavell calls 'openness through instantaneousness', which is another term for the candid.

Beckett's reading of *The Storm* is fascinating, not least for the way it arrives at a denial of the colour and energy that seems to be present. His first appraisal in mid July 1936 responded negatively to exactly this, sensing 'something almost like artificial excitement', and dismissing the picture as a consequence (Beckett, 2009, 359). But by August he had changed his mind, and 'liked it much better' (365). The process behind this reversal is revealed over a year later, in the more extended account quoted above. Here the 'artificiality' perceived in his first reaction has become a positive by being severed from any notion of a vitalistic 'excitement', and seen instead as akin to a theatrical backdrop: a 'nature almost as inhumanly inorganic as a stage set' (540). Beckett thus still sees nature as artificial. But, crucially, it is no longer *excited*. Rather, it partakes of the very different affects of the inhuman and the inorganic. These are the terms of mortification that recur in Beckett's public and private critical writing on painting and sculpture between the 1930s and the 1950s, together with allied adjectives like mineralized, remote, frozen, dead and immobile. Here, they serve to remove Yeats' painting from an initially perceived solicitous and importuning theatricality into something more akin to Manet's world of ennui and blank, mannikin-like posing. The title of the painting becomes ironized in this second take of Beckett's: here there is only a dreadful electric stillness through which we wait for a storm that never comes.

---

[3] I note here Roger Caillois's argument that 'the goal [of mimesis] is to become assimilated into the environment'. Beckett's attraction to the notion of the inorganic in art resembles Caillois's position in his influential 'Mimicry and Legendary Psychasthenia', an essay that also influences Adorno (Caillois, 2003, 89–107, 98).

The same feeling pervades Cezanne's landscapes, which in 1935 Beckett describes (approvingly) as 'an unintelligible arrangement of atoms'. He goes on:

> Even the portrait beginning to be dehumanised as the individual feels himself
> more & more hermetic & alone & his neighbour a coagulum as alien as
> a protoplast or God, incapable of loving or hating anyone but himself or of
> being loved or hated by anyone but himself. (Beckett, 2009, 223)

Here again one sees a parallelism between nature itself, depicted as a random, atomized scrim, the relations between people and other objects (i.e. protoplast and God) and the relations between one person and another (i.e. neighbours). The 'lack of rapport' within and between all of these elements is fundamentally the same. Which is also to say that there is no difference between any of them. God, mountain, human and protoplast inhabit a flat ontology, equalized through their common 'metaphysical separateness'. One can add to this, according to Beckett's comments on Yeats, the relationship between beholder and painting or, in Cavell's terms, between nature, the artwork, the audience and the individual.

It is the 'presentness' of Yeats' and Cezanne's paintings, the manner in which the canvas is made to face the beholder in its entirety, that attracts Beckett. This is also the thinking behind Beckett's later dismissal of Tal-Coat's painting as 'a composite of perceiver and perceived, not a datum, an experience' (Beckett, 1965, 102). Such a criticism is almost identical to Fried's strictures against the theatricality of minimalist sculpture in 'Art and Objecthood'. The main thrust of his concern is that it is the viewer's *experience* of the minimalist piece that is the aesthetic content, taking precedence over the artefact's own presence. Without the beholder's presence the object is simply a steel cube, or a grid of bricks. Such works are empirically registered objects, not artworks, without the aesthetic autonomy that demands acknowledgement (Fried, 1998, 148–72). Similarly, according to Beckett, Tal-Coat's adherence to the phenomenological vision of French modernism means that the painting is addressed to the beholder's *experience*, painted to be completed by an act of perception. A Tal-Coat canvas is a kind of rehearsal or staging of the coming-to-consciousness of an image under the ideal conditions of an artwork. Beckett's laconic description of Tal-Coat's painting as '[t]otal object, complete with missing parts' is a marvellously compressed summary of the goal of such art: the image is painted in such a way that it solicits or implies, and so in a sense already includes, the missing parts that the beholder's experience will bring to it (Beckett, 1965, 101). To put this slightly differently, such a picture is painted in the full knowledge and expectation that it will be completed by an act of cognition, and therefore continually addresses that act of beholding. There is no way that the painting can dissemble the fact that it was made to be beheld. It is inherently theatrical.

By contrast, when he is attempting to articulate what exactly he admires in Bram van Velde, Beckett emphasizes the autonomy of the paintings and their engagement with scepticism. In them 'the fundamental invisibility of exterior things [...] itself becomes a thing, not a simple consciousness of limit, but a thing that we can see and make seen, and make, not in the head [...] but on the canvas' (Beckett, 1983, 130). The 'consciousness of limit' referred to is the transcendental schema operative still in Husserlian phenomenology, the necessarily partial way we apprehend objects and the role of intention in completing the picture we have of the world. What Beckett calls 'a painting of criticism' – so emphasizing its Kantian assumptions – attempts to inscribe these limits with a view to demonstrating the active role of the beholder in completing the image (Beckett, 2011, 880). By placing the depiction of a 'fundamental invisibility' at the core of painting, van Velde speaks to Beckett's sense of the isolation and separation of all objects (God, mountain, human, protoplast), and makes it his task to find a positive material correlate for the inaccessibility of the thing. The key opposition between van Velde and Tal-Coat is thus that between a painting that is made 'in the head' of the beholder, and one that is able to convince that it is fully present and entire solely through what is 'on the canvas', even if there is no beholder. In essence, such a painting must convince us, must make us see, that it 'itself becomes a thing', in other words that it is as monadic and self-contained as the object it presents. It is not 'a composite of perceiver and perceived' because the perceiver, the beholder, the audience is ignored, abolished. Again, one can see the remarkable affinities with Cavell here: the 'fundamental invisibility of exterior things' is a core tenet of scepticism, and the idea that art can 'make it visible as a thing' recalls how Cavell sees *Endgame* reveal the brute metaphysical fact of separateness.

5 To-Be-Seenness: Fried and Film

Beckett's use of the off-screen voice V, who seems to direct the motions of the main on-screen character F, very directly raises the issue of what Cavell calls control. In other words, V accords with Cavell and Fried's conception of the role of the audience in theatrical artworks. By seeming to direct the action, V is participating in the scene, completing it, without ever being visible on the screen. To some extent she stands in for the audience, for what Fried terms the beholder, and as such she might be said to compromise the work's autonomy, or at least call attention to its limits. This might indeed be an example, then, of what Cavell calls the loss of the theatrical convention of candidness, and a concomitant need to control the understanding of the audience by including the latter as a carefully calculated perspective within the artwork. Such is

Courbet's anti-theatrical strategy, according to Fried, with the added factor that the beholder is also a stand-in for the artist himself (as 'first beholder') (Fried, 1992, 53–84). And there is clearly an element of authorial presence in V too, as she directs, or seems to direct, F in his movements.

And yet all this only serves to point up the capacity of F to withdraw into absorbed contemplation at certain other moments. It isn't a case of F having no trace of character at all, certainly if we see character as a function of depth, the implication of an inner life. Rather, the play relies on a sceptical impulse, the enigma of other minds, and finds all sorts of ways of staging this precisely as an enigma. The clearest example is the degree of F's absorption in the music as he sits listening to the cassette, head almost touching it, his face invisible, his hands tightly clutching the white machine. He is completely transported by the sounds to which he listens, and Beckett's play with the audience's access to Beethoven's music further draws our attention to F's aural experience. Indeed the enigmatic nature of F's inner life is a constant motif, mutely raised by gesture and expression at several key moments.

On the other hand, the extra-diegetic voice of V, with her litany of commands, suggests that F is a mere proxy, a puppet, himself a machine, an actor 'playing' a role, as the cassette plays a tape. At the very least V is able to predict F's movements, so that what we see on the screen has a habitual quality, as of a rote procedure, an automatism. And yet, in a further turn of the screw, this very sense of habit, of unthinking, mechanical activity, also partakes of total immersion in the task, the kind of candid obliviousness to the presence of an audience that both Cavell and Fried prize in an actor or depicted figure.

In this there is a parallel to Fried's recent reading of Douglas Gordon's 2003 *Play Dead*; *Real Time*, an installation featuring a film of a trained elephant responding to his off-screen trainer's instructions to lie down, play dead and get up again. As Fried puts it, citing Diderot, the earliest critic of theatricality in painting:

> Gordon's elephant Minnie may be described as absorbed in what she is doing. This is especially true in those stretches where she is lying on the ground and playing dead and then begins to make the seemingly enormous effort required in order for her to rise to her feet. Yet even once she is on her feet [...] our sense of the attendance to her trainer's instructions is very strong. Interestingly in this connection, Diderot noted that actors playing subordinate roles often did better in the sense of remaining within their roles than the leading actors, who, much to his disgust, consistently played to the audience. 'It seems to me that the reason for this is that [the actors in subordinate roles]

are constrained by the sense of someone who governs them,' he wrote. 'They address themselves to this other, toward him they orient all their action.'

(Fried, 2011, 171)

This is very suggestive indeed in terms of understanding the complex play of relationships between V, F and us as viewers. Crucially, for Fried the sense that the elephant is 'attending' to instructions does nothing to detract from our sense of her absorption in her task, indeed it seems to intensify it. Candidness or absorption is reinforced through inclusion of an author–director–beholder (the trainer; V) within the scene.

Fried argues that Gordon's film is an example of the emergence of a new paradigm in the problematic of absorption and theatricality 'starting in the late 1970s' (Fried, 2011, 170). My wager is that this concern also emerges in Beckett's play of the exact same period, but that it builds on concerns in his work that go right back to the 1930s. Understood in this way, the presence of V as author–director acts not only to order the character to perform, as previous interpretations have argued, but also to self-consciously elicit a certain mode of absorbed acting, a performative approximation of sheer happening, Cavell's 'occurrence'. Further, I suggest that V's function as implied beholder, and her relations with the actual beholder (we the viewers), continues the Beckettian experiment with audience that Cavell first identified in his essay on *Endgame*.

A final word before we move to a close analysis of the play. *Ghost Trio* is a television play, designed to be encountered on a screen. As such, it exists in an entirely different medium to those works we have so far considered, apart from the Douglas Gordon piece. There lies the rub. For both Cavell and Fried, painting and theatre on the one hand, and film on the other, assume entirely different and incompatible relations with their audience. Owing to the material basis of photography as an automatic registration of light, a film presents a world replete in itself, entirely sequestered in the moment of its creation. As such, the actors unproblematically retain that candidness that Cavell finds to have disappeared from the theatre. As a result, the question of theatricality simply does not arise. A character in a film cannot break the fourth wall and address the audience. If they do so, they are simply addressing the wall itself, the ontological barrier that *screens* them, in both senses of the word. This impossibility of theatricality is the reason for Fried's notorious statement that film cannot be a modernist art. Modernism, for both Cavell and Fried, is constituted through the repeated attempt, from Manet onwards, to *defeat* theatricality, so that if the latter is simply not possible in a given medium, modernism is impossible too.

How is it, then, that Gordon's *Play Dead*, an installation composed of two large screens on which Minnie's performance unfolds, can be understood as engaging with the modernist *agon* with the theatrical? And by extension, how can *Ghost Trio*, as a TV play, be caught up in the same quarrel? Fried himself has said that he still sees the account of film and theatricality in 'Art and Objecthood' as broadly correct. In his 2011 book *Four Honest Outlaws: Marioni, Ray, Sala, Gordon*, however, there is an attempt to nuance that position. Here it is argued that Gordon's piece, and other video works by Anri Sala, rather than employing absorption as a strategy against theatricality, take the relationship between these two tactics as a subject. More specifically, he argues that Gordon and Sala are concerned with 'the empathic-projective mechanism that lies at the heart of one's response to often minimally expressive absorptive motifs' (Fried, 2011, 198). Fried's term for the staging of this mechanism, the specific tactic used by film and photography to examine theatricality and absorption, is 'to-be-seenness'.

Empathic projection is another Cavellian notion, found in *The Claim of Reason* (Cavell, 1979a, 421–5). For Cavell, such projection is the means whereby one can inhabit the perspective of another, and so combat scepticism; it is the ability to see what another person means, to break the shell of the solipsistic. For Fried, classic absorptive motifs in painting rely on this facility, exploiting it in the struggle with theatricality. That is to say, the absorptive artist relies on a beholder's ability to imaginatively project rich textures of experience onto the very subtle cues supplied by 'minimally expressive' motifs of dreaming, vacant, absorbed faces and postures. In doing so they undergo an aesthetic experience of a latitude and depth that overpowers the thin melodrama of the theatrical.

Yet, if Fried still maintains that film is intrinsically non-theatrical, then the destruction of theatricality cannot be the impetus behind the use of absorption by Gordon. Rather, it seems that contemporary gallery films and video installations take absorption as an object of enquiry, a convention, and stage its operation in order to dissect it. In doing so, they rely on the cinema's privileged relationship with candidness: as Fried puts it of a 2000 piece, *Déjà-Vu*, for example, a work where Rudolph Mateé's 1949 film noir *D.O.A.* is projected on three parallel screens at slightly different speeds, here Gordon 'use(s) [. . .] movie-acting as an "ontological object"' (Fried, 2011, 210). This is an art that carries out a challenge to, and calculated examination of, Cavellian candidness in acting. The mystery of absorption, and of the projective empathy that undergirds it, is thus tested not by theatricality in the classic sense, which importunes, solicits, overwhelms, is mannered and false, but by what Fried calls a 'laying bare'. In doing so, he is clearly concerned with distinguishing the video art he admires from the theatricality of some post-war art:

> The notion of a laying bare of empathic projection may seem to imply an appeal to the viewer's 'experience' in the Minimalist/Literalist sense of the term, but [. . .] I do not think it does. Rather the force of that laying bare is structural, intentional, almost abstract; it is a specific effect, built into the work, and in principle is the same for all viewers. (Fried, 2011, 177)

The minimalist/literalist position is the one attacked as theatrical in 'Art and Objecthood', where the artwork assumes the presence of, and demands participation by, the beholder as individual. This is the disposition criticized by Cavell in 'The Avoidance of Love', when he describes how 'each man is revealed privately, for there is no audience, apart from each man's making himself an audience [. . .] each man has his reasons, good or bad' (Cavell, 1976b, 346). Such a solipsistic position cannot access the *sensus communis*, the a priori principle of every judgement of taste, the urge to share and acknowledge aesthetic judgements. By contrast, Fried sees Gordon's work as presuming an audience rather than a set of atomized experiences; its effects are 'in principle [. . .] the same for all viewers'.

As we have seen, Cavell associates the diminishment of the tragic aesthetic with the saturation of the contemporary broadcast media-field with theatrical images of pain and suffering. The question of how theatricality can function so effectively in such a context, given that photo-journalism and TV are, like film, screen-based (and therefore, according to both Cavell and Fried, inherently non-theatrical), is not really addressed by Cavell. Perhaps the nature of television's reception – its consumption in a domestic setting – and the rhetoric of 'live' news reportage are powerful enough to counter cinematic ontology. In any case, the conventions of installation works like Gordon's are clearly closer to the condition of film than TV: large, often multiple screens, rear-projected images, in the public space of a gallery or museum setting. And yet Gordon seems to at least nod to domestic media through the inclusion in the installation of a television monitor, on which the most directly affecting – and theatrical-seeming – element of the work appears: a melancholy close-up of Minnie's eye (though this also seems to be a homage to a very similar shot in Bresson's *Au Hasard Balthasar*). Although Fried doesn't mention this, it is another aspect of the way *Play Dead* investigates the nature of absorption, pitching the unblinking, suffering, solicitous gaze of the animal on the small screen against the gargantuan efforts of absorbed performance on the large.

Play Dead raises many of the sorts of questions that I want to pursue in *Ghost Trio*: the nature of performance in the absence of character; the role of the author–director–beholder; the resistance of absorption and the beguilements of the theatrical. Like *Play Dead*, *Ghost Trio* is also clearly bound up with form: it is, in Fried's terms, 'structural, intentional, [...] abstract'. With its strange grammar of shot and repetition, the play not only invites the viewer's absorption, but stages absorption and questions it, in the way that Fried associates with what he calls 'the to-be-seen' (Fried, 2008, 58–9). At the heart of both works is an extraordinary performance that questions the very notion of acting. As a non-human animal, Minnie seems to achieve the kind of performance that Kleist dreamed of, that of the dancing bear, and it is useful to consider an audience's reaction to F in *Ghost Trio* in the light of it. Minnie has no character to disappear into, and yet she is certainly performing, acting. That performance is, however, dependent on the instructions from her trainer. There is a very strong sense that this is also the case in *Ghost Trio*. When Minnie plays at being dead, she becomes a kind of ghost, and Pickup was also instructed, by Beckett himself, to in effect play dead, to abandon the conventions of the human for something else (Knowlson and Pilling, 1979, 279). The inhuman, whether as doll, puppet, animal or artwork, has always been implicated in the limits of empathic projection, and so of the depiction of absorption. Cavell calls this limit the 'seam':

> If I stopped projecting, I would no longer take anything to be human, or rather I would see no radical difference between humans and other things. I am, after all, very selective about this already. Only a small proportion of the things I see, or sense, do I regard as human (or animated, or embodied). Projection already puts a seam in human experience; some things are on one side of the seam, some on the other. (Cavell, 1979a, 425)

And some things are on the seam itself, or cross it continually only to come back again.

6 Resorting to Rectangles

Ruby Cohn recounts a remark from Beckett on the genesis of *Ghost Trio*: 'I wanted a calm scene which revealed an inner storm as the camera approached, but the figure resisted me, so I resorted to rectangles' (Cohn, 2005, 339). I will be returning to this gnomic statement frequently in what follows.

The play opens with a perspectival, black-and-white view of a small room, a cube or cell, the walls and floor receding evenly, so that the viewer is immediately placed in a commanding position and remains fixed to the same spot for most of the Act. The point of view is neither high nor low. Nothing moves. It is as if one is looking at a still image, in painterly terms an interior (Figure 2).

all luminous, faintly luminous.

Figure 2 Beckett, *Ghost Trio*, BBC, 1977

The 'resort to rectangles' that constitutes Beckett's reaction to his difficulty with F is already present here in this first shot, in its hard-edged frames, the shapes and surfaces that surround the hunched figure. Clement Greenberg famously stressed the basic structural support of the picture as a means of delimiting the aesthetic concerns specific to painting as a medium (Greenberg, 2002). Similarly, Beckett's appeal to the rectangle is a way of reaching for painting, and its philosophical resources, as a means of coming to terms with the enigma of the figure he creates. It is a means of translating an impasse into an enabling condition. For it is by drawing on the concerns of painting, and its preoccupations with perception, the materiality of the art object, the role of the beholder, absorption, theatricality and anti-theatricality, that Beckett investigates and foregrounds the recalcitrance of F to his imagination, making of it the focus of the play.

The idea of placing a seated, absorbed figure in the mid-ground before a window or door, so that the window forms another framed image behind them, in a recessed space with other echoing rectangular shapes, is a very familiar device in western art, particularly of religious visions, visitations, annunciations. Giotto's *Joachim's Vision* is one intriguing antecedent here. The idea of an annunciation is of course germane to *Ghost Trio*: as mentioned earlier, the play turns on the idea of a tryst, an assignation: F, we will eventually discover, is waiting for someone. But it is the juxtaposition of the absorbed, enfolded, enswathed figure of Giotto's Joachim and the strict, black rectangle of the doorway behind him that carries the most weight as a point of comparison.

Another set of pictorial references can be drawn from the Dutch and Flemish art that so attracted Beckett (Knowlson, 2009). The juxtaposition of window and single absorbed figure is a familiar device in seventeenth-century genre painting. Here, the characteristic format of the annunciation is secularized, with the attendant angel replaced, more often than not, by a letter. Vermeer's *Girl Reading a Letter by an Open Window* is probably the best-known example, though pictures by de Hooch, Elinga and Jacobus Vrel also take up the theme. Indeed, *Ghost Trio* seems to explore a very similar territory to Vrel's sombre, subdued, brumous images. His enigmatic *Woman at a Window, Waving at a Girl*, hanging in Paris in the Fondation Custodia, is particularly suggestive, given the striking image of the child in Act III.

An important variation on the Dutch development of figures and interiors is the use of images of music-making to suggest the kind of transportation, intensity and internal reflection (or the potential for such) that supernatural emissaries had once provoked. Pictures by Vermeer (*A Young Woman Seated at a Virginal*; *A Young Woman Standing at A Virginal*, both in the National Gallery in London, and *The Guitar Player* at Kenwood House) and Gerrit Dou (*A Lady Playing a Clavicord* in Dulwich) are relevant here.[4] Beckett's inclusion of a figure whose air of absorption is focussed on music from a tape recorder again allies the scene with such a painterly heritage.

All of this demonstrates that the opening Act of *Ghost Trio* can be located within a painterly tradition of composition. The single-point perspective as a means of organizing and manipulating the gaze, the stillness of the scene, the maintenance of the camera at eye-level, all encourage the notion that our relation to the screen is that of beholder and painting.

After thirty seconds a voiceover begins, listing the objects in the room and their generic qualities: 'the familiar room', 'the indispensable door', 'a kind of pallet', and so forth. This may be why the first act is described as the 'Pre-Action'. The scene sketches the necessary co-ordinates for dramatic action, or to put this in more Kantian terms, the necessary conditions of dramatic experience. The a priori form of space, and the concepts that the understanding applies, are emphasized at the expense of the intuition and sensibility

---

[4] Beckett knew all these pictures from his year in London in the mid 1930s (see Carville, 2018, 2–3).

that give body to them. Hence, perhaps, the dim, faded, hushed, feeble tone of the proceedings. The light is uniform, V tells us, bathing all equally, so that there are none of the shadows that might give a sense of material bulk and weight.

V is also at pains to point out that she is impervious to a specific quality of objects, and in particular aesthetic objects: their affective properties, their ability to evoke mood, feeling and emotion:

> I. I. Good evening. Mine is a faint voice. Kindly tune accordingly. [Pause] Good evening. Mine is faint voice. Kindly tune accordingly. [Pause] It will not be raised or lowered, whatever happens.

In other words, this is a voice that will not react, will not allow itself to deviate from its even, purely descriptive tone. Such dispassion seems to tally with the way the whole scene is calculated to play down sensual, sensible description: the faint light, the lack of shadow, the colour grey.

This, then, is what the stage directions and diagram call 'the general view', from camera position A. As viewers, we automatically assume that the voice we hear is also issuing from this spot, looking at what we are looking at. The very fact that the source of V's speech is invisible encourages us to do so. In effect, her perspective and ours coincides: like us she is a spectator, a member of the audience. And yet she also addresses herself *to* us, like a television announcer. Thus the locus of her perspective is split from the very first moments: looking in as beholder, addressing us as guide.

In this way, V does not seek to ignore the fact that an audience is present (nor, as we shall see, that the audience has a potential agency). The audience becomes, in effect, part of the artwork, in a manner that can be called, with Cavell and Fried, theatrical. We are explicitly involved through V's address, given a role, even a specific attitude ('kindly tune accordingly'). Indeed, such 'action' as there is in Act I, the series of close-ups of the objects in, and components of, the space, is motivated solely for the audience's benefit and cannot be understood without the notion of an external gaze to which it is being offered.

This is not to say that the scene is wholly theatrical, however, for the beholder is also, in many ways, frustrated, shut out, in effect ignored by the images on the screen: closed window, closed door, muted colours, evenness of lighting, not to mention the nature of the eventual 'resort' to the still, inset rectangular images of the floor and the wall, to which we will be returning. And of course there is the figure of F himself, absorbed in music that we cannot hear until the end of the scene. As viewers we are, in the way that Fried remarks of Gordon's *Play Dead*, both solicited and challenged.

The way in which Act I of *Ghost Trio* immediately pitches notions of interiority and opacity against ideas of the address to, and the participation of, the audience confirms the play's relevance to Fried's account of the history of anti-theatricality, coming between modernism's reworking of the problem of the beholder and the more recent emergence of the problematic of 'to-be-seenness' in photography and artists' films. In this context, Beckett's desire for and inability to access the forms of interiority, of 'inner storm and calm scene', as he puts it to Cohn, registers the waning of the conventions of classical absorption. By the same token, his 'removal of "character" for the actor to disappear into' (in Cavell's formulation) is a response to this loss. If the 'internal' storm cannot be revealed, there is no character, and thus nowhere for an actor to go. There is only 'acting', acting purified of character, in the same way that Kleist's puppets are purified, or his dancing bear. Or Minnie the elephant in *Play Dead*. Onto what, Beckett asks us, can the audience project, in such a situation? With what feel empathy? It is the same question Manet poses in *A Bar at the Folies-Bergère*. The resort to rectangles will explore this question across the whole duration of the play.

In line I.2, V says: 'Forgive me for stating the obvious'. This comes after she has described the light and the colour of the scene. It is the anxious admission of a certain superfluity to her presence, and again transfers agency to the beholder. The viewer does not need V's commentary, we can clearly see the calm scene being described, though V needs the viewer's indulgence. Having said that, a statement of the obvious is entirely germane, in that it establishes the import-ance of sheer surface at this early point in the play, counterpointing the notions of depth, penetration and revelation that will later come into focus. What is obvious to the eye, absolute fidelity to appearance, to *happening*, is in fact V's special realm. All she does is describe, seemingly unable to do anything else, and it is this that the plea for forgiveness is designed to stress. She will continue to gloss what we could see and understand unaided for most of the scene. Except for the case of one word, *Dust*, which is not at all a statement of the obvious.

Previous interpretations of *Ghost Trio* have automatically assumed the dom-inance and control of V (Herren, 2007). But if this is the case it is curious that she feels it necessary to ask our forgiveness, or inform us of her independence, saying further in I.2 that her voice will be 'neither raised nor lowered', so that we must 'tune accordingly'. Again, it has often been pointed out that these are self-reflexive moments, drawing attention to the volume settings of the televi-sion and the material form of the broadcast medium. In keeping with Fried, however, I prefer to think of them as theatrical, an appeal to the beholder and a recognition of the latter's collaboration, or participation, in what is going on. It is here that the distance from film becomes important. The reference to the ability of the viewer to engage with the television marks a very specific relationship with the beholder, one that compromises any notion of there being an ontological 'abyss' between the viewer and the world on the screen in the sense that we find in Cavell (Cavell, 1979b, 229).

But here I want to concentrate on the strange echoes of the word 'kind' throughout the Act. 'Kindly' is repeated twice at the start, at I.2 when the viewer is asked to tune themselves to the play. Then, shortly after this, there is a reference to 'some *kind* of pallet'. This is picked up in the repeated lines that accompany the 'rectangles' that appear between I.3 and I.27, the close-ups of the objects in, and aspects of, the room: 'the *kind* of wall', 'the *kind* of floor', 'the *kind* of window', 'the *kind* of door', and so on. In a scene of such brevity and linguistic economy, this repetition cannot be accidental. But what should we make of it?

'Kindly tune accordingly.' In the first place, this phrase admits that the voice's authority, its ability to communicate whatever it has to say, is dependent on the collaboration of the viewer, but that this collaboration is not limited to the mechanical act of tuning in a receiver. In fact that act is explicitly forbidden by V, so we are talking about something rather different here. The rhetoric of kind and kindliness that Beckett deploys implies the notion of empathy, an idea also there in the reference to tuning, attunement (which in turn suggests an important link to the use of music in the play). The German word *Stimmung* captures this more accurately. This is a term with a long philosophical history. Cavell uses it with a Wittgensteinian inflection: 'our ability to communicate with [another] [...] depends upon our mutual attunement in judgements. It is astonishing how far this takes us in understanding one another' (Cavell, 1979a, 115).

Similarly, in *Ghost Trio* the viewer is expected to respond 'in kind' to the faint voice, the faint colour, the abstracted images, the spectral, mute world with which they are presented in Act I. We are to be kindly in the sense of accommodating themselves to the mise-en-scene's delicate, tentative tonality. This is not an easy task. The voice's deliberate faintness, and seeming refusal or inability to increase in volume, demands the supplement of an active subjective tuning, an imaginative labour that cedes an active role to us, the viewers. Prevented from adjusting the sound, we must focus, strain to hear, concentrate, we must become absorbed. We adopt the position of the figure that we watch on the screen. Listening intently. Indeed, the first snatches of music that we hear are themselves faint, and we must tune in delicately to these too. If V's address to us is theatrical, it is a theatricality that invites absorption.

It is true that we, as viewers, can refuse to perform this kind of tuning. We may instead simply turn the volume up (even easier now than when *Ghost*

Trio was first transmitted), controlling the voice ourselves and destroying the spectral atmospherics of the piece. To do so would clearly be contrary to the effects that V desires. Hence again it is not a case of the viewer simply completing the work in a theatrical way. The viewer must also adapt to the work, abjuring a control that is always temptingly available ('keep that sound down') in favour of making present the other, however faint and tenebrous. The work comes first, this is the main lesson of the imperious voice, and the distance of key aspects of the play from conventional theatricality – its to-be-seenness – derives from this.

Act 1 also sees a counter-movement to this strain of attunement and absorption, however. One that registers the ever-present potential failure of absorption that Beckett alerts Cohn to. The idea of a calm scene and an inner storm might be a definition of Fried's notion of absorption: the creation of a pictorial image that implies emotion, deep inwardness and profound depth of feeling, but does so without the least direct address to the viewer. Beckett's admission of his 'resort to rectangles' is both fascinating and valuable, however, for the way it implies that Act I's repeated use of highly formal, abstract close-ups is in some sort of important relationship to the resistance of *Ghost Trio*'s enigmatic central character to the audience's apprehension. On five occasions in Act I the stage directions specify a close-up of a rectangle, corresponding to floor, wall, pallet, window and door (Figure 3). In each case the camera cuts directly from the general shot of the whole room to the close-up. On the other hand, lines I.31–3 stipulate that the final close-up of F's head is the result of one prolonged movement from the position general view at A. 'to close-up of head, hands, cassette. Clutching hands, head bowed, face hidden'. This extended movement thus enacts an approach that seems to promise access, but ultimately ends in obstruction. It is the kind of movement that sponsors absorption's combination of insight and mystery. Beckett's statement suggests a dissatisfaction with the recalcitrance of F's absorption. And the implication is that he turned to the rectangles out of this frustration, so that they embody or instantiate his (and our) lack of access to F. And yet he also seems to suggest they are an alternative to absorption, another form of it, a resolution of some kind to the issue of access. Certainly the highly abstract images are difficult to grasp, but, if we conceive of them as a kind of preparation for the closing approach to F's bowed head, the terms of Act I become slightly clearer.

This relationship between the rectangles and F is confirmed by another, more formal and technical set of comments that Beckett made on the play as an aid to its realization. This contains a series of paragraphs providing advice on staging and costume etc. One of these is headed 'Camera':

Figure 3 Beckett, *Ghost Trio*, BBC, 1977

> Once set for shot it should not explore, simply stare. It stops and stares,
> *mainly in vain.* Its mobility is confined to stealthy or lightening (cut shots)
> advance or withdrawal to positions established in view of the most telling
> stills. Exceptions: 1) Recording from C of F moving from door to window,
> window to pallet, pallet to stool. 2) Close up of pallet, object of a special gaze.
>   (Beckett, 1976b)

The first striking thing about this paragraph is the reference to 'staring' that is
mostly in vain. There is a clear continuity here with the remark that F somehow
'resisted' Beckett during the process of composition. It is another indication that
resistance to depiction, and the problems and aesthetic opportunities this occasions, became integrated into the play. Beckett writes himself into the play,
taking the place of the beholder, dramatizing his own relation with his subject-
matter. In Fried's terms, Beckett deals with the historical failure of absorptive
convention, and the consequent threat of theatricality, by usurping the place of
the beholder himself (this, as we have seen, is the Courbet solution). Another
aspect of the 'camera' passage reinforces this suggestion. The 'lightening (cut
shots)' it refers to are the 'rectangles' he mentions to Cohn, while the 'stealthy
advance and withdrawal' is a clear reference to the three sequences where the
camera slowly moves in on F as he sits on the bench beside the door. The
association of these two opposing tactics in the note, and their distinction from

the exceptions (1) and (2), suggest there is an important relation between them. What they share, it seems, is the sense of 'staring in vain': both dramatize, in their differing ways, a moment of resistance to the gaze.

Between I.2 and I.6 V tells us first to look, then 'Look closer', and as the close-ups first of floor and then of wall appear, intones one word: 'Dust'. Then, between I.6 and I.28, the play cycles twice through a series of close-ups, not only of the wall and the floor but also of the window, door and pallet. Accompanying these shots the voice now intones: 'The kind of wall'; 'the kind of floor', 'the kind of pallet', etc. The strong implication is that the beholder will synthesize the single word 'Dust' on the soundtrack and the two close-ups of wall or floor on the visual track to make a cognitive judgement, and eventually formulate a series of propositions. The kind of floor is a dusty floor, the kind of wall is a dusty wall. After each cycle through the close-ups, first of wall and floor, then of wall, floor, window, etc., at I.28 V enjoins us to 'Look again', and we return to the position general view. Now, the implication is, our grasp of the state of affairs as a whole has been altered by the judgement we were encouraged to make earlier, when we synthesized dust with wall and floor.

In effect we have been supplied with an empirical assessment of the room, and this in a very specific way. The means of arrival at the claim or proposition that the kind of room is a dusty room is classically rationalist. Subject and object remain at a distance; though the object is scrutinized closely it is through conceptual templates, theoretical modes of grasping the real rather than a practical phronesis. Understood in this way, the rectangles of Act 1 attempt to enact visually, in an aesthetic context, a cognitive procedure, a judgment that is not itself aesthetic. That is to say, the ostensible purpose of the business with the rectangles and close-ups in Act 1 is to facilitate a determinate judgement: this room is the kind of a room that is dusty. Inasmuch as it does this, then we do not participate in the free play of the faculties that Kant locates at the heart of aesthetic experience. In Cavell's terms, this is an experiment in knowledge rather than acknowledgement.

And yet, once we actually attend to the close-ups as visual images, we find that this is not quite true. The beholder's experience is actually profoundly aesthetic, and has been calculated to be so, in a way that accords with the spectral mood to which we have been enjoined to attune. The close-ups are almost completely flat and abstract. They consist, in the case of the wall and floor, of light grey rectangles on a slightly darker ground, although the very relationship between figure and ground is a debatable one.

The serial, repetitive nature of the shapes is also disorienting, and runs counter to the idea that we are being schooled in an act of empirical reasoning.

Beckett is extraordinarily careful in specifying the exact shape of the letter-box specimens of floor and wall that appear, clearly intent on ensuring that they are as close to the same size as possible. Hence the sections of floor and wall, and the whole window, are all specified as rectangles of the dimensions 0.70 × 1.50 metres, while the pallet and door are both 0.70 × 2.0 metres. Where the perspective of the general view addresses and situates the beholder firmly, inviting us in, the close-ups, when they come, rebuff us. It is difficult to get a purchase on them: they seem designed to emphasize the flatness of the screen on which they appear rather than constituting it as a transparent window, in the way the general view does.

As these two factors might suggest, the upshot of this combination of word and image is not a more detailed, empirical account of what is seen. Despite the way that V explicitly uses the resources of television – sound, image and their conjunction – to address the beholder, despite her confident assertion that we have now 'seen it all', the actual experience is rather more perplexing. For although we are exhorted to look closer, the image is markedly undifferentiated, giving no real purchase for vision. Again, the directions in the script emphasize this: wall, floor, window and door are all described as 'smooth grey rectangle[s]', while the window is an 'opaque sheet of glass' and the pallet a 'grey sheet'.

More than this, however, there is a sense of the defeat of theatricality, one that issues here in a series of images that have their own strange grace. V's attempt to co-opt the beholder's cognitive response to the close-ups is at odds with the indeterminacy of the images on screen. The austere, perplexing autonomy of the first two, the framed images of wall and floor, in particular create a dissonance that will shudder through the whole play. The close-ups form a set of barriers to the beholder, the wall and floor like blocks of mist or scumble, the door and window closed. Flat and resistant, their rhythmic appearance dominates the first Act and signals through their resistance their independence from, and indifference to, both V and the beholder. It is in this that they anticipate the encounter with F that immediately follows.

This sense of the close-ups as both a frustration and enactment of a basic cognitive process is reinforced by the way that V accompanies the first two close-ups, the framed sections of wall and floor, with the same single word, 'Dust'. As Ruby Cohn points out, the viewer cannot in fact see this dust. It is invisible (Cohn, 2005, 338). And yet the word suggests the terrain of material ruination and atomization that has been Beckett's image of the non-human real since the mid 1930s. In *Texts for Nothing VII*, the speaker waits 'for day to break behind the locked door, through the glass black with the dust of ruin' (Beckett, 2010, 32). In *All Strange Away*, a text close in its hermetic setting to *Ghost Trio*, a woman lies 'left breast puckered in the dust' (Beckett, 2010, 78). But it is perhaps throughout *Fizzle 7: For to End Yet Again* that we find the most overt description of dust as representative of a completely inhuman terrain: 'Sand pale as dust ah but dust indeed deep to engulf the haughtiest monuments which too it once was here and there. There in the end same grey invisible to any other eye stark erect amidst his ruins the expelled'. Or again, 'Grey cloudless sky ocean of dust not a ripple mock confines verge upon verge hell air not a breath. Mingling with the dust slowly sinking some almost fully sunk the ruins of the refuge' (Beckett, 2010, 151).

V's repetition of the word 'dust' further moves the scene away from the empirical and the cognitive into an aesthetic realm that is attuned to the tentativeness and spectrality of the Act as a whole. As viewers, we are given the form of a determinate judgement, supplied with both the sensuous material of the image (grey rectangle) and the concept (dust), yet they seem insufficiently aligned, each somehow in excess of the other, so that the judgement becomes reflective, purely formal, without purpose or end. The understated, austere combination of monochrome and monotone complements the liminal flickering of the faculties as the beholder probes the work. In this way, we are far from André Bazin's modernist idealization of the power of the camera in his 1945 essay 'The Ontology of the Photographic Image': 'Only the impassive lens, stripping its object of all those ways of seeing it, those piled-up preconceptions, that spiritual dust and grime with which my eyes have covered it, is able to present it in all its virginal purity to my attention and consequently to my love' (Bazin, 1967, 15). For Beckett, dust, far from being the impurity to be cleansed, is itself the essential though indiscernible thing, the Schopenhaurean zone of dissolution and destitution that glimmers beyond the Kantian – or any other – schema. In this it is a variation on the other images of dessicated materiality that we saw emerge much earlier in his writing: atomization, petrification, the inorganic.

As a consequence, the sense of the revelation of dust as object of knowledge in Act I is not a wholly critical or ironic move, though there is certainly a dimension of this. That is to say, on one level we might interpret the whole business of the close-ups as a kind of sceptical allegory: here is what your rationalism reveals, the merest husk of life. And yet in the light of the modernist conventions of absorption and acknowledgement at work in the play, we might also see a dialectical revaluation of the standard devices of theatricality here. Just as Manet deploys the explicit address to the beholder, yet moulds it to a new anti-theatrical art, so Beckett deploys the techniques of rationalism but forces them to a point of revelatory aporia that is aesthetic rather than cognitive, a reflective judgement rather than a determinate one. It is aesthetic in that it is not offering to the audience a fact of knowledge ('this room is a dusty room') but an incitement to acknowledgement ('you are looking at a work of art'). In this way, Beckett's resort to rectangles marshals both direct theatrical address to the audience ('look [...] look closer [...] now look again') and the practices of empirical observation in the service of a vision that, far from confirming the beholder in a position of control, presents them with the pure presentness of images that look, for all the world, like the kinds of canvases Fried and Cavell were finding equally 'instantaneous' in New York in the mid 1960s. As with Manet, theatrical means are tasked with anti-theatrical ends.

All of this is thrown into context by the rest of the act, which seems to dramatize what Beckett meant when he spoke to Cohn of the 'resistance' of the figure at the heart of his proposed scene of turmoil and calm. In this respect, the long, stealthy shot that closes in on F's head and face between I.31 and I.35 parallels the previous close-ups of the other objects in the room (Figure 4). Indeed, the earlier part of the play – which is otherwise very difficult to account for – seems designed to pre-empt and complicate any complacent understanding of our relation to F in conventionally absorptive terms. This is especially clear when one notes the use of music across the Act.

The first hint of Beethoven's Fifth Piano Trio, the beginning of bar 47 of the Largo, emerges 'faintly', as the script specifies, at I.13, accompanying the close-up of 'the whole door. Smooth grey rectangle [...] imperceptibly ajar'. It then

Figure 4 Beckett, *Ghost Trio*, BBC, 1977

comes back, as the beginning of bar 49, at I.23, when, after the series of close-ups of window, pallet and window again, the camera returns for a close-up of the door once more. The effect of the latter is intriguing when compared to the way the other still images are accompanied only by V's voice or silence. The addition of music deepens the image of the closed door, despite its planar, perspectiveless nature. One suspects that the music is coming from behind the door (though it is eventually revealed that it is issuing from the cassette recorder in F's hands), and as such it promises an access to depth. The door is thereby distinguished as a privileged topos in this space, and the play's use of music here seems quite familiar, more akin, indeed, to a cinematic soundtrack than a play, televisual or not.

The music is then absent until I.31 to I.34, and the final camera movement from position general view A through points B and C to the close-up of F's head. Now it is the beginning of bar 19 of the Largo that we hear, and it grows slightly louder at each successive point. Then, when the camera withdraws from the close-up back through C and B to A again, the music slowly diminishes. Both these moments thus associate the music with proximity to F, and in doing so subjectify the camera. That is to say, the beholder moves with the camera into the space of the room, closer to the music, which gets louder as a consequence. To put this another way, the camera is embodied. As a result, the flat, two-dimensional frontality of the play up to now is definitively superseded. We are in F's space, close to him, and we can hear the music he is listening to, share it, though his face is still 'hidden'. We can also see, by the time the camera reaches I.32, that he is holding a cassette recorder, from which the music must issue. As the camera returns to rest at A again, F remains in his absorbed, listening pose, suggesting that the music continues, though now we cannot hear it. The diegetic source is thereby emphasized again. To some degree, then, the music is F's, situated beyond the perspective point at A, which we associate with V, who does not refer to or address it at all in Act I.

All of this serves to lend the end of the scene a new sense of access to F and also a sense of naturalism. We can hear ambient sound, the sound of the room, as opposed to the voice of V, which the music serves to contrast with. Where V is impassive, Beethoven's music is turbulent and moving. Where V's voice is never raised or lowered, the Largo varies in volume depending on our proximity to F. Compared to the stern experiment of the close-ups of the floor and wall etc., the slow movement in to F, with its accompanying music seems a relief, holding out the promise of inwardness, absorption.

And yet at the very same time all of these aspects, which seem to alleviate the austerity of the previous theatrical address, are themselves highly theatrical, and revealed to be so. To take the music as an example, what initially seemed to be a token of mystery and passion is eventually concretized in a mundane diegetic source. Its effects are artificial, engineered, granting only the illusion of access to the other through a time-worn romantic trope. The notion that there is an essential accord, an immediate and necessary isomorphism, between the increasing 'storm' of the music and the inner experience of F is a convention that we assume with no evidence. The fragility of the convention may also account for, and give real substance to, V's insistence that we 'keep that sound down': for such manipulation of the volume would shatter the careful way that the music is calibrated to distance, bodily presence and excessive emotion. In this and other ways it is as if we are going through the exhausted motions of conventional absorption. And yet at the same time the procedure is still undeniably effective. In this way Act I both exercises and undercuts the conventions of the depiction of absorption.

7 'He Will Now Think He Hears Her'

If Act I prepares the scene by requiring the viewer to attune themselves to a condition of faintness and indiscernability, and to acknowledge the pertinence of the conventions of theatricality and absorption, Act II changes tack abruptly. V now makes a series of statements that hover ambiguously between orders to F and advance descriptions of his actions. In any event it is hard not to interpret the relationship between V and F as causal, which raises the question of how that causality is effected. If F hears V and responds, then they occupy the same world, in the roles of author/director and character/actor. Alternatively, if V's voice is heard only by us, as audience, the two characters do not inhabit the same continuum, with V being sequestered on 'our' side of the ontological divide. There is thus no causal relationship, F is unaware of V, and V is a viewer who can anticipate what F will do. In this case V's stance is theatrical, offered to the audience; in the former case it is much less so. Once again, conventions of address are foregrounded.

In Act II, F moves around the space, opening the door on the right and the window at the back, staring down at the pallet and looking in a mirror on the left wall. The viewer's sense of being impeded from access to F continues: Beckett is careful to note, very early on in F's circuit of the room, as he 'turns still crouched to door', that we only see a 'fleeting face'. Elsewhere, as F moves around the cube, inspecting door and window, Beckett specifies that he always stands with 'back to camera'. For the most part, the camera stays at position general view, although at one point, about two-thirds of the way through, it repeats the movement last seen at the end of Act I, moving in to a close-up of F's head bent over the tape recorder.

In contrast to these attempts to complicate or preclude empathic projection between the viewer and F, V describes both the physical, visible events that take place on the stage, and also the affects and percepts experienced by the central character. Hence V's first words, at II.1, are 'He will now think he hears her', and F looks up towards the door to his left, as if startled by a noise beyond it. The phrase suggests that V is now able to do more than 'state the obvious'. It is not immediately apparent that F is mistaken, that he has imagined the noise. Without V's comment we, as audience, would have no inkling of this possibility. As it is, when F subsequently starts, and raises an arm, we already *know* that he is reacting to an event that only happened in his imagination. The play then relates the consequences of this virtual event: the listening at the door, the opening of the window, the opening of the door, etc. V either has knowledge of F's mind, or directs him to behave as if she had.

Similarly, the narrator intones the same two words: 'No one', at once describing the absence of sound and presumably the empty views through the window and door, though the viewer does not see this, only F's back as he opens each and peers out. To assert this, therefore, is to claim to know what F sees and hears. This is to detach, a second time, the voice from the general view, the central perspective that we, as viewers, are still forced to occupy. The image track and the soundtrack diverge: right from the start of Act II, in other words, V and audience begin to be forced apart. The corollary of this is that the general gaze is supplemented by another virtual scene, one that does not appear on screen but that V can presumably see, whether from some vantage point alongside F or through somehow occupying F's subject-position. For the audience's part, watching F's back from our general vantage point at A as he pushes the shutter open and leans out into the void, we see only the resistance of the grey, stark, feeble image before us, the long grey cloak, the back of the head. As beholders we, the audience, are excluded from the narrative, as we were from the images of dust during Act I. V's voice is offering us the view, however, and as a result the statement is addressing us, sketching in what F sees, though only in the most rudimentary way. It is a theatrical address, but a remarkably opaque one. Fried's term 'to-be-seenness' is appropriate here once again. It is thus no coincidence that the structure of this moment echoes precisely the two disorienting close-ups of floor and wall in Act I.

The relationship of beholder to image, and the mediating role of V in that relationship, thus changes significantly in Act II, and this is stressed by structural parallels of word and image between Acts I and II. The beholder is no longer addressed, indeed ordered, by V to look; rather, the focus is on V's knowledge of F's interiority. There is, in other words, an explicit overcoming, or at least the construction of a fiction of the overcoming, of the problem of other minds, of scepticism. The strategy of 'to-be-seenness' now explicitly engages with, or lays bare, the structure of projective empathy. This change is demonstrated if we compare V's 'stating of the obvious' in Act I with what is happening in Act II. For now *it is precisely what is occluded from us that is being described*, namely F's internal life, or V's understanding of it. The emphasis has moved from what can be seen to what cannot be seen or known. Similarly, where in Act I the beholder is directly presented with a series of opaque images that rebuff interpretation – the blank rectangles of floor, wall, window, etc. – here, although we are given a set of resistant, dorsal images of F as he looks out of the door and window, the viewer is provoked to provide their own moments of imaginative insight, as V intones what is, or appears to be, seen (Figure 5). The effect is to suggest that V occupies the perspective of F, even as we the viewers are excluded. This is emphasized by the way the words 'No one' are spoken while F stands 'back to camera' at II.8 to II.11 and II.16 to II.17. Even as we seem to occupy F's position through empathy with or attunement to V, we are barred at the level of the visual. Such moments bring together absorption and theatricality in an anti-theatrical moment: we see the classic dorsal image of F, and are enjoined to imagine what he sees, and yet what he is seeing is purely negative: 'No one'.

Figure 5 Beckett, *Ghost Trio*, BBC, 1977

This structure of F looking, with V glossing, is reversed a little later:

II.21. F *turns to wall at head of pallet, goes to wall, looks at his face in mirror hanging on wall, invisible from* A.
II.22. V [*Surprised.*] Ah!

The mirror is a real, material object that presumably bears a virtual image (i.e. a reflection), but it does not form a part of the general view from camera position A in Act II: the audience can only see its right-hand edge. And yet, strikingly, despite this invisibility, F's look into the mirror elicits a gasp of, and Beckett's directions are specific, 'surprise' from V. Here we remember the opening statement of Act I: V's voice 'will not be raised or lowered whatever happens'. The pact that was established between V and the viewer in Act I, where the latter was importuned to 'kindly tune accordingly' to V's faint voice, is now broken.

What is the reason for V's surprise? Given that this look in the mirror is the first action by F that V has not ordered, or described in advance, the assumption must be that it is unexpected. Previously, V seems to be directing F's actions to some degree. This is especially apparent from the way that the stage directions specify F stand 'irresolute' at each stage of his journey from door to pallet etc. before V describes his next action. It is as if F is waiting for a command before proceeding. The word 'irresolute' disappears in the stage directions accompanying the move to the pallet when F 'stands looking down at it' for five seconds. The loss of the figure's irresolution, and the absence of any description or command by V, renders F's action more independent. There are other changes too at this point. When F looks at the bed at I.20, V does not say 'No one', as she had when he looked out of the door and window. The implication is that something is seen or experienced in the course of the gaze on the pallet. As before, the audience sees only an occluded view, the crown of F's head as he bends to look. Yet the absence of either voice or music renders the moment intensely private in a new way: there is none of the overcoming of scepticism implied by V's previous statements. We sense the aura of an inner life without any address to us that might frame or otherwise focalise it. Soon after this, the audience's relationship with V also changes. When F looks in the mirror and she gasps, the sound is not a gloss or supplement to F's mental state in the manner of the earlier declarations that there is 'No one' at the door or window. It certainly accompanies F's action, but it does so as reaction, as happening, rather than anticipation, switching the temporality of the relationship: the positions of cause and effect are reversed.

It is V's gasp that now betrays the kind of theatricality previously seen in F's startled raising of the head at II.2. If we follow the thought that V is a stand-in for the author, who has made the resistance of F the fulcrum of the play, then V's gasp can be interpreted as another moment in the thematization of that core concern, though the exact import of this will only become clear in Act III. At this stage suffice to say that V's gasp is clearly involuntary. As such, it no longer addresses us as beholders, it no longer has designs on us. It becomes part of the scene depicted, rather than an external commentary upon it. It is, in Cavell's terms, *candid*. It confirms that V no longer occupies position general view A, alongside the beholder, for there is, I suggest, the implication that V has been somehow discovered. While there was 'no one' behind the rectangles of door and window, the rectangle of the mirror reveals the 'her' of V, if only through a gasp.

This then seems to have consequences for the rest of the scene. V's next utterance, 'Now to door', is ignored by F, who instead returns to his seat, and the sequence of shots from I.31 to I.35 – the progression of the camera from A through B and C to a close-up of F's bowed head and back – together with swelling and fading music, is repeated. In other words, we have a collapse of V's theatrical address to the beholder, and instead an image of intense absorption coupled with the return of a competing form of theatrical address, that of Beethoven's Largo. As in the same sequence at the end of Act I, then, a complex assemblage of shots concerning looking, accompanied by V's voice, is followed by a lengthy approach and withdrawal together with music that suggests conventional absorptive effects.

In the sequence of approach and withdrawal to F that ends Act I, it is stipulated that there is nothing audible from A, the general view, and this is true also of the same movement as it is repeated between II.26 and II.30. This changes at the very end of Act II, however, at II.35, when Beckett stipulates that the music is 'audible from A for the first time'. Now the music is detached from its ostensible source in the cassette and functions to colour the scene in the manner of a soundtrack, rather than as an element of the diegesis. What is more, for the first and only time in the play, V refers to the music and seems to assert her control over it. 'Stop', she says, and the music does. Here, for the first time, the extra-diegetic voice of V and the sound of the music clearly occupy the same space, and seem to be pitted against each other. Even so, this development marks an important second instance, after V's exclamation at II (itself, as we have seen, diegetic), of what seems to be a challenge to V's authority, or at least a new departure, a variation, that she does not initiate and is concerned to arrest. At this point V has resumed her position of power over the scene, and her last word, at II.38, is 'Repeat', which seems to point forwards to Act III, when all of Act II is indeed rehearsed again. The significance of this moment, just as important as V's cry, will also only become clear in the course of Act III.

8 Objects of a Special Gaze

In Act III, the general view from A does not feature at all. Instead, we see a series of near, close-up and, in an important development, several point-of-view shots that align us with F himself, bringing the viewer into close proximity with his experience through the use of the camera. Another departure is the complete absence of V's commentary. We seem to have moved from Act I's formal framework, which encouraged identification with a seemingly objective look from outside the diegetic space, to a transitional position in Act II, where the beholder, F and V are involved in a play of absorption and theatricality, to a final stance in Act III where the beholder is (mostly) firmly located alongside F.

One consequence of all of this is that the final Act is much less rebarbative that the previous two. Rather than a play of identification and resistance, we have a relatively traditional narrative, one that employs cinematic conventions in familiar ways. We are also allowed to perceive rich and subtle sense impressions while the camera occupies F's point of view. Hence, when the corridor that stretches off behind the door is finally revealed at III.9, the view ends in deep shadow, clearly contradicting V's prescription that there be 'no shadow' in Act I. Similarly, the point-of-view shot that accompanies F when he looks out of the window at III.16 sees rain falling dimly, and is accompanied, crucially, by its sensuous patter. This use of diegetic sound continues throughout the Act. When F closes the door, there is a dramatic, indeed over-dramatic, creak. Also, Beethoven's Fifth Piano Trio is much more prominent on the soundtrack than previously. Thus, the first shots of Act III – near shots and close-ups of F crouched in absorption over the cassette – are rendered much less resistant than the equivalent shots in Act II by the way Beethoven's music is permitted to resound. We are thereby exposed to what we know by now to be the aesthetic experience that F himself is undergoing, so gaining a privileged access to his consciousness. Another major factor is the absence of V's voice, and its replacement by sound effects at key moments. These sounds – the opening and closing of a door, the sound of rain, footsteps – are indexically linked to on-screen images, and thus explicitly located in a way that V's voice was not. They serve the action, are not disjunctive, do not insinuate an indeterminacy between themselves and the performance. As aural cues they facilitate our attunement to this world, but in a different manner to V's voice. In this way they can be allied to the much greater role that music plays in Act III. In addition, the camera now occupies the 'position near shot' C for the most part, much closer to F, and there are several point-of-view shots from F's perspective, immersing the beholder for the first time in his perspective. Finally, the rectangles of Act I return, though as we shall see they are strictly governed by a new regime, one that conditions and is conditioned by the point-of-view shots.

The first shot in the whole play that is clearly and conventionally located in F's perspective is at III.9, the view through the door after he opens it, for the first time, to see if anyone is there. We have already seen this moment, but from the general view at A in Act II. Now, however, it is shot from much closer, at C, and with a soundtracked creak indexed to the action:

> III.8. *Crescendo creak of door opening. Near shot from C of stool, cassette,*
> *F with right hand holding door open, 5 seconds.*
> III.9. *Cut to view of corridor seen from door. Long narrow (0.70 m) grey*
> *rectangle between grey walls, empty, far end in darkness. 5 seconds.*
> III.10. *Cut back to near shot from C. of stool, cassette, F holding door open.*
> *5 seconds.*

Note here the visual rhyme with the 'rectangle' close-ups of Act I: the width of the grey rectangle between the grey walls is the same as that of the floor and wall sections of Act I. Line III.11 continues the same shot as III.10 for another five seconds, as F removes his hand from the door and it closes with another creak. This is followed by a '*cut to close-up from above of cassette on stool, small grey rectangle on larger rectangle of seat*', which is in turn succeeded by a return at III.13 to the same shot as III.10 and 11: a near shot from C of the stool, cassette and F standing at the door.

In effect, between III.8 and III.13 we have three almost identical images of F shot from the same position at C, interrupted by two very similar 'rectangle' shots from radically different points of view: the first clearly from the subjective perspective of F as he looks down the corridor, the other of the cassette on the stool from what seems to be a completely objective position, unattached to any previous gaze, unaligned with any of the three camera positions given in the script (Figure 6). This is something that the shot shares with the close-ups of Act I, and like them it is composed of rectangles. In this sequence, the default camera position of most of Act III from C is thus momentarily displaced first by a completely subjective shot and then by what seems to be a completely objective shot.

It is this section of the play that Beckett specifies, in his 'Camera' note, as an exception to the 'staring in vain' of the camera in the rest of the play, creating instead a sense of 'exploration'. This exception is thus not achieved by the automatistic 'stare' of the camera being filtered or adjusted in some way. Rather, the distinctive feature of the sequence is the consistent rhythm of subjective shot and objective shot that begins with the moment I have just identified. The articulation of objective and point-of-view shots sets up a new relationship with the beholder. As we saw in Act I, the rectangular shots of floor, wall, door,

Figure 6 Beckett, *Ghost Trio*, BBC, 1977

window and pallet came one after the other, were accompanied by V's voice, and were abstract, planar and two-dimensional. In Act III, by contrast, the dominant sense is of an embodied looking. As Beckett specifies in the stage directions, the rectangular shot of the corridor at III.9 is a 'view': there is a strong sense of depth, generated through the insistence that the far end of the corridor be in darkness. This lures the eye rather than barring it: there is always the possibility that something might emerge out of those shadows. And this is intensified by the arrangement of the other two shots in the cluster, placed before and after the 'view'. Both are of F, holding the door ajar and looking, which implies that the view they bracket is his, that we have adopted his gaze and are looking through his eyes. This is what Beckett must mean in his note by the new sense of exploration at this point. And it also seems that the 'resistance' of F has to some extent been overcome. We seem to be able to comfortably, and somewhat suddenly, overcome our scepticism and occupy his perspective.

Or have we simply slipped into a theatrical mode, and are now being co-opted by formal manipulation? Certainly after the strange and challenging play with the viewer of Acts I and II, this moment is very a conventional positioning of the viewer. To adapt Cavell, suddenly everything becomes relevant, unavoidably so. That is to say, the ability of the audience 'to make present' is not being taxed in the way it had been earlier in the play. The suspicion that Beckett is 'quoting' conventional theatrical practice here, as part of a larger anti-theatrical strategy, is further provoked by the 'crescendo creak of the door opening' that accompanies III.8. This explicitly diegetic sound is certainly theatrical, melodramatic even.

At this point, however, the next rectangle – the shot of the cassette recorder – is cut in, so that the embodied view is challenged by something else, something stranger and less immediately intelligible. Beckett's direction here clearly locates the image of the cassette alongside both the view through the door and the abstract cut-ins of floor and wall of Act I, all shots that have the structure of grey rectangle on grey rectangle, although he does not specify the dimensions of the cassette.

There seems to be no narrative motivation for this image. It is not seen from the point of view of F for example, for the two shots that bracket it make clear that he has his back to the stool and cassette. It is also distinctively different in texture and mood from other relevant surrounding shots. The light grey colour contrasts with both the preceding view down the shadowy corridor and the subsequent view out of the window at the rain. Similarly, both the door shot and the window shot employ diegetic sound and F's point-of-view shot. And both induce a sense of 'exploration' in the viewer that could be seen as deploying theatrical convention. That is to say, their perspectives draw the beholder into the piece, and into F's perceptual field, staging it as an experience one can share, promising revelation with a veil of rain, creaks and shadows. But the creak and shadow, the return of perspective, the careful preparation of a place for the beholder to occupy, tends to a theatricalization of subjectivity. We do not *earn* our occupation of F's gaze; we achieve it through convention, one that has been exhausted through repetition, not least by televisual narrative.

The tape recorder, by contrast, is empty of function, mute and impenetrable. As such, it seems to intensify the deadpan, transcriptive quality of the camera. This is for several reasons: the contrast with the relatively lush image of the corridor it is paired with; the way the stark geometry of the machine harks back to the austere images of the close-ups of Act I; the abrupt, non-motivated nature of the cut; and the fact that the machine is mute (especially coming so soon after the exaggerated creak of the opening and closing door). It is all object, so to speak, without anything by way of music or voice to gloss it, despite its function being to bear sound. Rather than the theatricality of an image soliciting and securing a beholder, it offers reflexive consideration of the conventions of both theatricality and absorption. The image of the silent cassette, with its suggestion of aesthetic experience withheld, coupled with uninflected material presence, thus exemplifies 'to-be-seenness'. As such, it announces a series of such images that counterpoint the images of 'exploration' in Act III.

Before turning to those images in detail, it is worth recalling Cavell's description of the silent alarm clock in *Endgame* here: 'Hang the run-out object where art used to hang, for if only art is worth looking at, nothing is. Hang it up because it is a real thing, empty of function and alarm; and in the place of art, which is not able to recover' (Cavell, 1976a, 153). It is fascinating to consider this statement in the light of Fried's criticisms of minimalism in 'Art and Objecthood'. Like the minimalist object, the alarm clock in *Endgame* is a real thing that takes the place of art, a nihilistic (in Fried's view) coda to the tradition. Cavell's contrast and connection between the empty, redundant object and the artwork might also be applied to that between the mute cassette recorder and the embodied or theatrical view of the corridor that preceded it. Like the minimalists, Beckett does seem here to posit a kind of pure, material objectivity as an ultimate resort. The rest of the sequence will continue to negotiate between the idea of a literal object and the conventions of both theatricality and absorption.

The five rectangles or close-ups in the sequence following the image of the corridor through the open door are: the cassette from above; the view through the window on the rain; the pallet from above; the empty mirror; the face in the mirror. Each is bracketed by two shots of F in the same position. In other words, there are six couples of identical shots of F, one before and one after each close-up. Six groups of three shots, then (though one of these, at III.23, acts as the final shot of group 4 and the first shot of group 5), all exhibiting the same structure: shot from C/still or objective shot/repetition of shot from C, right up until III.28.

Thus, for example, as F goes from the door to the window we have:

III.15 *Near shot from C holding window open.*
　III.16 *Point-of-view shot of rain falling.*
　III.17 *Near shot from C holding window open.*

The combination of near shot from C and narrative action as F moves around the room contributes to the more naturalistic sense of exploration that Beckett specifies in the manuscript advice should be absent elsewhere in the play. Remember that V is not present at all in Act III, so that the conventional assumption that F is carrying out an intentional action is not compromised by her anticipations or initiations of his movements ('Now to door' etc.). This, coupled with the intimate but not overly intrusive shots from C, give F's circuit of the room a much less artificial tenor. The near shots from C, coupled with the physical movements of F, allow a momentary weakening of the play's strict abstraction, as the viewer is interpellated, provided with access to a standard narrative perspective that is sometimes close to F's own and at others identical with it. Yet, as with the cassette close-up isolated above, seeded through this more narratively conventional sequence are a series of important shots that recall the close-ups of Act I.

This brings us to the second exception to the camera's 'stare', as recorded in Beckett's instructions: 'pallet: subject of a special gaze'. When F reaches the pallet we shift from the view from C to again briefly occupy the fully sub-jectivized gaze of F, and so see exactly what he sees, from his point of view, as he looks down. Beckett specifies that the bed is of exactly the same dimensions as the window: 0.7×2 metres. In this way it is another iteration of the rectangle motif that was established in Act I. The manner in which Beckett specifies that the object is shot from above also associates it with the image of the cassette recorder that is cut in thirty seconds earlier.

These point-of-view shots of the pallet – III.20, III.21 and III.22 – are bracketed by two shots that explicitly locate their 'special gaze' as being from F's perspective. Thus III.19 repeats, using a near shot from camera angle C, Act II's direction 20: '*V goes to head of pallet (window end), stands looking down at it*'. Subsequently, we have first the shot of the pallet from above: '*Cut to close-up from above of whole pallet*'. Immediately after the shots of the pallet from above, the camera cuts back to F, still with his head bowed: 'near shot of [. . .] F, head of pallet. 5 seconds'. Following this a close-up of the empty mirror intervenes, another rectangle shot, succeeded by a five-second shot of F from camera position C, still looking down at the bed (and thus not at the mirror, to which we will return in a moment).

The stage directions explicitly state that F is looking down from the head of the pallet, and this is where he stands in the BBC version. And yet when the pillow appears it is shot from the side, in order, I suggest, to facilitate the tracking of the camera which, in the script as published, follows the initial shot of the pillow, at III.21 (Figure 7). This movement is more than likely the 'special gaze' that Beckett mentions in his instructions: the camera was to 'explore' the pallet, moving slowly across its length from the pillow to the foot and back again. This is what happens in the German version of the play, though it was lost from *Ghost Trio* for reasons of time (Cohn, 2005, 338). Accordingly, in *Geistertrio* F stands by the side of the pallet, rather than at its head (contrary to the script), so that the discrepancy between the position of F and the lateral movement of the point-of-view shot of the pillow is resolved. This change confirms, if such confirmation were necessary, that the shot of the pallet is a subjective one, cued to the point of view of F, repeating the shots of the corridor and the rain slightly earlier in the Act. The difference from those two shots, however, is that this is not a view of the outside of the room. Rather, the image depicts an object, barring our view, and in this sense speaks back to the still of the cassette recorder. Or rather, it combines the objectivity of the view of

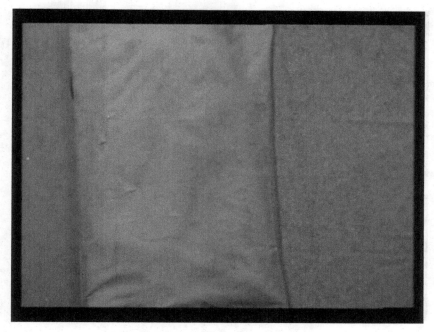

Figure 7 Beckett, *Ghost Trio*, BBC, 1977

the cassette recorder with the subjectivity of the views of the outside. That is to say, its objectivity is compromised by its clear positioning as a point-of-view shot, while its subjectivity is thinned-out due to its unmotivated quality, the lack of the goal that animated the searching glance out of the door or window. The nature of the gaze is opaque: the sense is one of absorption, as with F's immersion in music, but the blank surface of the pillow yields no clue as to why it might provoke such a fascination. We inhabit the seam of the subjective/ objective dichotomy, as if Beckett is again aiming at the Kleistian quality of Act II, although this time attempting to somehow inhabit the marionette, to see the pallet through eyes that are absorbed, but not in a human way.

It is now, immediately after the gaze on the pallet, that the mirror is given to us for the first time (Figure 8):

> III.24. *Cut to close-up of mirror reflecting nothing. Small grey rectangle (same dimensions as cassette) against larger rectangle of wall.*

The directions here – 'same dimensions as cassette' – again suggest a formal link to the tape recorder shot, and as with that image, Beckett distinguishes the mirror-shot by stressing that the perspective upon it *cannot* be F's. As noted already, the shot of the empty mirror is succeeded by another five-second shot of

Figure 8 Beckett, *Ghost Trio*, BBC, 1977

F from camera position C, still looking down at the bed. The bracketing structure thus permutates the procedure that framed the previous subjective shot of the corridor. In that case, the shot from F's perspective was preceded and followed by a shot that demonstrated the subjective nature of the gaze they bracketed. By contrast, the shots of F that flank those of the cassette and the empty mirror demonstrate that the gaze on these images cannot be subjective.

The shot of the empty mirror also recalls the series of abstract cut-ins of Act I. Like them it consists of a rectangle within a rectangle, is shot straight on, is symmetrically structured and bears a frame where the earlier shots had a suggestion of one. Similarly, the Act I close-ups drew attention to their own flatness and abstraction, as contrasted with the view of the room from the position general view, and so too does the shot of the mirror. The major difference, and development, from the Act I close-ups, however, is that that the mirror is specified as 'reflecting nothing'. This suggests that the beholder, or the place of the beholder, has now been erased from the diegetic scene. To put this another way, where Act I explicitly acknowledges the beholder, through V's exhortation to 'look' and 'look closer', in the manner that Fried terms theatrical, Act II does not. Instead, we simply have the blank rectangular image, a framed void that, in the scandal of its emptiness, renders the very existence of a beholder who gazes upon it questionable. The fact that it is reflecting nothing also suggests a parallel with the mute cassette. Both pieces of equipment are not carrying out their intended functions of recording or representation, but are themselves being pictured solely as dumb material objects.

What happens next is thus all the more striking. Five seconds later, the camera returns to the mirror:

> III.27 *Cut to close-up of F's face in mirror. 5 seconds. Eyes close. 5 seconds. Eyes open. 5 seconds. Head bows. Top of head in mirror. 5 seconds.*

Now we seem to have another clear point-of-view shot (the contrast with the previous mirror 'reflecting nothing' is calculated to emphasize this). We are seeing F's reflection as he looks in the mirror, occupying his position, for the first time, as beholder of a representation, rather than a gaze upon an object or an outside view. We are also now beholding the mirror as bearer of an aesthetic image, for the image of F's face is extraordinarily affecting, concentrating all the pathos of the classic close-up. The texture of the lined, marmoreal face and the liquid, gleaming eyes create a powerful juxtaposition with the variously resistant, abstract or calculatedly objective close-ups we have previously encountered.

We remember too from Act II that this is the moment at which V exclaims in surprise, leaving behind the affectless demeanour that we associated with the mode to which we are called to 'tune' in Act I. Is it too much to say that V now also beholds this image of F's face? It is true that her gasp is not present in Act III, but the scene is calculated in such a way that we are bound to recall it: we might say that we are still attuned to that gasp. Thus the audience, as beholder, is returned for an instant to her point of view. We see what she sees, though we do not hear her gasp. This provokes a further consideration, that of the exact point at which V's gasp issues. For as Beckett's directions at III.27 make clear, F's look into the mirror is composed of three stages: the initial look, the closing and opening of the eyes, finally the bowing of the head. Given that V's exclamation comes at the central point of the play, and we have now established that this central passage has three stages, is it perhaps the middle stage of III.27 in particular that provokes the gasp from V? I am referring here to the couple of seconds where F closes his eyes.

9 The Face of the Father

In support of such an interpretation we might recall the description of the father's face in Beckett's 1946 short story 'First Love'. The narrator is describing, or trying to describe, the face of a prostitute who has accosted him:

> As to whether it was beautiful, the face, or had once been beautiful, or could conceivably become beautiful, I confess I could form no opinion. I had seen

> faces in photographs I might have found beautiful, had I known even vaguely
> in what beauty was supposed to consist. And my Father's face, on his death
> bolster, had seemed to hint at some form of aesthetics relevant to man. But the
> faces of the living, all grimace and flush, can they be described as objects?
>   (Beckett, 1989, 22–3)

I have argued elsewhere that this passage is a kind of primal scene for Beckett's
aesthetics, one that dramatises an enduring though often re-examined set of
concerns: the fate of beauty in modernity, the question of the very possibility of
aesthetic judgement, the spatial nature of visual form as opposed to the temporality of the word, the authenticity of sensuous perception, the link between
representation and death (Carville, 2018, 6–9). Beauty is here a property of
objects, the dead and the photograph, all of which are seen as removed from the
'grimace and flush' of organic life. We are back in the terrain of petrification,
familiar from the letters on Cezanne, Jack B. Yeats and Watteau. But there is
also a striking similarity to the following passage from Henri Fantin-Latour's
correspondence, which Fried cites as a key absorptive trope. The painter is
writing in 1875, after witnessing the death of his father:

> I didn't see any trace of consciousness, everything was internal but reflected
> on his face, then came a state which I can't describe, lightning-flashes that
> passed across his face, a succession of different expressions; intelligence
> took the place of imbecility, he became grave. Oh! it was admirable,
> I watched for several minutes the greatest spectacle one can see; I never
> stopped saying, 'Oh! how beautiful it is, how beautiful it is.'
>   (Fried, 1999, 251)

Fried comments: 'What impressed and moved Fantin, it appears, was the
combination of absolute absorptive closure ("I didn't see any trace of consciousness") and the height of expressiveness, instantaneousness, and strikingness' (Fried, 1999, 251). The combination is different in Beckett's case, in that
the last flash of vitalism, the 'succession of expressions', is definitively absent.
But the anti-theatrical combination of 'absolute absorptive closure' and theatrical 'strikingness' is the same nevertheless.

Here I want to pause to consider Beckett's reference, in the quote from 'First
Love', to the 'death bolster'. It is a strange locution, but one that can help us to
understand something of the significance of that mysterious 'special gaze' that
Beckett talks about in the manuscript of *Ghost Trio*. For it is above all a bolster –
that I want to think of as a death bolster – upon which the gaze of the camera
concentrates in III.21.

In the light of the image of the face of the dead father in 'First Love',
Ghost Trio's linked shots of pillow, cassette recorder, mirror and the image
of F's face at III.27 form a significant complex. The still of the pillow can

be conceived, like the mute cassette and the empty mirror, as depicting a ground with no figure. It is a form that does not bear the content that might be looked for in (or on) it, the missing content being, in the case of both the mirror and pillow, the face or head that might expected to be found there. It may be, then, that F, by searchingly looking at the pillow for an extended period, is attempting to imagine something very specific: his own head, resting on the bolster, asleep or perhaps dead. After all, the indications are that this dusty cell is his, the pallet his bed, and so if the stills are connected through some kind of missing element, then F's own presence would seem to be the most obvious candidate. The juxtaposition between empty pillow at III.21 and blank mirror at III.24, the latter seeming to await the presence of F's face, which eventually enters the mirror at III.2, reinforces this reading, as it is surely designed to suggest that the pillow is missing the face, just as the mirror initially is. Further, it is immediately after looking at the empty pillow that F hastens to the mirror (so breaking with his previous obedience to V's injunctions). Once again, we might interpret this movement as a reaction to the failure of the pillow as ground for an image, and a compensatory desire to produce such an image in the mirror. F, then, first looks for, imagines, his own dead face on the pillow, and then produces it in the mirror by facing it and closing his eyes.

We can now recall the moment in Act II when V says 'Now he will think he hears her', though we are not given the imagined footsteps or knock. Or when she says 'No one' as F looks out of the window and we see only his back. Here, by contrast, we are given a view of the pallet but there is no gloss, no 'No one'. When we see the actual view out of the window earlier in Act III it is glossed with the rich, sensuous sound of rain, inflecting the image. But here we have no guide. What is F's absorbed look seeing? Is he seeing what we, as audience, see (i.e. the empty pillow)? Or something else? We cannot know, and this taint of scepticism qualifies the notion that the shot of the pillow is a subjective one from F's point of view, moving it closer to the objective pole occupied by almost all the other rectangle close-ups. The camera is able to mimic the movements of F, and register the external screen on which he projects his own images, but does not inhabit his picturing gaze, thus excluding us, acting as much as a barrier as a portal.

Immediately after the final close-up of the pillow, F turns to the mirror. This is then followed by:

> III.27. *Cut to close-up of F's face in mirror. 5 seconds. Eyes close.*
> *5 seconds. Eyes open. 5 seconds. Head bows. Top of head in mirror.*
> *5 seconds.*

The cut from III.26, where F is seen to go to the mirror and look in it, to III.27, which Beckett explicitly states is a '*close-up of F's face in mirror*', strongly encourages us to see the latter as a subjective shot, from F's point of view (Figure 9). Where else could such a perspective be located if not in the point of view of the character who has just approached the mirror? But in fact, as becomes clear, we are not inhabiting his point of view. For when F shuts his eyes the scene does not fade, rather we continue to see the image that F cannot now see. Our address to it has changed. We see it from the outside, so to speak, our position no longer identified with that of the image it bears.

It is here that the prior shots of the cassette and the empty mirror come into conceptual play. As pointed out earlier, both mute cassette and empty mirror are shot from predominantly objective positions. These shots are the most detached in the play, shot from unidentified locations, devoid of any contextualization or motivation through montage or sound, and unanchored in the subjectivity of F. Like the rectangular close-ups of wall and floor, they resist the beholder through their lack of inflection and the way they place the beholder at a strict distance from the world of the play. Now, however, the beholder is given absolutely no theatrical assistance from V in apprehending them, is locked out from them in the same way they ostentatiously refuse their usual functions of representation. The face we see is clearly a rejoinder to these grounds without figures, these blank objects, so much being strongly implied by the prior inclusion of the contrasting objective shot of the mirror reflecting nothing. As such, they should be regarded as extremes against which the relative inflection or colouring of all other shots should be assessed.

Figure 9 Beckett, *Ghost Trio*, BBC, 1977

With this in mind, we can grasp another aspect of the image of the face. The closed eyes suggest it cannot be subjective, and yet, as with the pallet, the gaze does not feel objective either. This is in part because the point of view plays with a recognizable and familiar vector, that of a look into a mirror, in a way that no other close-up does in the play. Thus, initially, the camera seems to register the reflection of F's face after his turn to the mirror, and we as beholders occupy his position. In effect, we assume F's stance as he examines his reflection, becoming one with him as he looks, and so crossing the boundary into the film-world, rather than keeping our distance.

But when the eyes close, this assumption becomes untenable. There is now only one place from which this shot can be recorded, and that is from the point of view of the mirror itself. We are not, or rather no longer, looking from F's point of view, but from the point of view of the recording mechanism (the mirror, but also, by extension, the camera). And yet, even so, the moment has none of the chilly abstraction that the close-ups of mirror and cassette exploit. This is partly because of the sheer, almost overwhelming pathos of the face, but also due to the careful constellation of close-ups I have been tracing. As beholder we are within the world of the film. Or perhaps more accurately, we are in a position right on the border of the film-world, occupying the surface of the mirror in which F looks, troubling the distinction between objective and subjective shots. In this sense we remain caught up in the subjective gesture of looking, albeit from the opposite side of the glass. And indeed, despite the closure of the eyes, it remains very difficult to shake the notion that we are still involved in a conventional, familiar specular relationship with our own reflection. We thus stare back both from the position of beholder and from the place where the image of F is inscribed: we occupy a position that is fully both objective and subjective. In this way, the close-up of the face speaks across the whole play, unifying it by calling to mind a whole series of objective, rectangular close-ups, but also exploiting the several previous moments of subjective point-of-view shots.

Such a moment might be called theatrical in Fried's perjorative sense. F's long look directly into the camera, his finger pointing to his eye, directly engages us as beholders, pinning us to a particular subject-position. The trace of V's gasp in response to F's look at II.22, hovering in the background here, reinforces this aspect, for as we have seen she is a character who, amongst other things, stands in for the beholder. Her gasp is our gasp now, and the strikingness of the face is certainly capable of eliciting one. And yet this moment is also very clearly circumscribed in multiple ways that suggest an intention to steer it away from any such simple exploitation of direct address to a beholder. Fried says of Manet's bold, front-facing figures that in painting them the artist was not simply adopting an actively theatrical mode but presenting theatricality itself. Beckett's procedure here has similar hallmarks. These include: a clear suggestion that F is regarding his own image, rather than an audience, and is absorbed in it; the way it is implied that the image on the screen is being seen from the point of view of the mirror itself; and the structural association of the face with the empty pillow, mute cassette and blank mirror shots. In other words, it is not that F importunes us or panders to our gaze in a theatrical manner. Rather, what we have is a kind of reflexive absorption, an absorption that takes the otherness of one's own face as its object, a tradition with a long history in the self-portrait. The viewer takes part in this moment by occupying the place of the object that register's F's face (the mirror), by becoming the image at which F looks and by being placed at F's point of view as he looks in the mirror. The viewer puzzles through all of these possibilities. Theatricality is thrown into disarray by being rendered as a component of self-inspection, just as the very possibility of absorption is compromised by the emphasis on exteriority. In this reading, it is the undecidable play between the dyads absence/presence, imagination/reality, death/life and subject/object that precipitates F's departure from the previous pattern of causality in the play.

In the aftermath of this sequence, which begins with the view down the corridor and climaxes in the mirror-shot, the nature of the whole play changes. It becomes much more conventionally graspable in its narrative structure, generic in its sound effects and predictable in its unfolding. It is almost as if, after the scepticism of Act I, and the disjunctions of Act II and the first half of III, there is a kind of return to order. Even so, anomalies remain. Thus another version of the ambiguous gaze, neither securely subjectively determined nor completely objective, and not theatrically positioned, is also present in the scene that, in purely narrative terms, would seem to be the climax of the play. This is the moment when both F and the audience hear a knock on the door and footsteps approaching, with F opening the door a second time to see the young boy who looks up at him and wordlessly shakes his head (Figure 10).

Once again, Beckett's directions are precise: 'White face raised to invisible F', he says of the boy, indicating that F is out of shot and therefore that the boy's face should not be raised directly to the camera. During the whole shot the boy looks up and to the left, indicating that the viewer is not occupying F's point of view, as we had seemed to be in Act II, when F looked down the empty corridor. Instead, we are level with the boy's face and he seems to be looking somewhere above us to our right. In this shot, in other words, the camera is again inflected with an independence from conventionally theatrical or interpellative positions. This slightly skewed relationship with us, coupled with the contrast to the earlier subjective shot down the empty corridor, creates a displacement between

Figure 10 Beckett, *Ghost Trio*, BBC, 1977

us as beholder and F as beholder, prizing open our identification with F even as the boy acknowledges him.

The boy closes his eyes slowly twice as he twice shakes his head, recalling F's own action as he looked in the mirror at III.27, and this double gesture of negativity, together with the paleness of the boy's face and the blackness of his cowl, suggest death and deathliness. Indeed, we might say that the shaking of the head *refers* to the closing of the boy's eyes, and thus to the previous closing of F's eyes. In other words, the boy's message, relayed in a kind of dumb-show, is that death (the closing of eyes) will not come tonight (the shaking of the head), despite F's earlier fantasy of his own finitude. Thus, as with the scene of F's face in the mirror, the shot of the boy's face offers a momentary glimpse of an aesthetics relevant to man, and this time, unlike previously, F is able to behold it, although we do not see him do so, nor does the boy address his gesture directly to us as beholders. This is indeed the climax of the play, the dialectical resolution of all that has gone before.

10 *The Ghost*

At the beginning of Act III the music takes the place of V's voice, and is used, rather oddly and non-naturalistically, to counterpoint other aspects of the sound design. It is audible right at the start of the Act, but then stops abruptly at III.3 and again at III.6, when F raises his head as if he has heard something from behind the door. We can clearly see the cassette recorder in his hands, and the implication is that he has paused it or switched it off (in *Geistertrio* this is made explicit, as Klaus Herm's long, bony finger taps the side of the cassette recorder). Similarly, towards the end of the play at III.30, when footsteps from behind the door appear on the soundtrack, the music that had been playing for ten seconds abruptly stops to allow them to be heard. In between these two moments there is no music at all, but instead a series of diegetically located sounds: the creaks of the door as it opens and closes (twice), and the sound of heavy rain outside the window.

All this has a bearing on one of the Act III close-ups that we have already mentioned. This is the shot, from above, of the cassette recorder at III.12, an image flanked by two shots of F standing at the door, his back to us and the cassette, which we can see on the stool. The first of these two flanking shots differs from the second only through the movement, and the sound, of the door closing with a 'decrescendo creak'. This emphasizes the silence of the cassette shot when we move to it immediately afterwards. The image of the silent machine also contrasts strongly with the powerfully sensuous image of teeming rain, accompanied by the equally lush sound of its falling, that we see from F's point of view when he opens the window. The silence of the cassette recorder image, the disjunction between visual and sound image, serves to point up, by negation, the way the music is now being used predominantly as a narrative device rather than an aesthetic object facilitating F's absorption.

Hence the importance of the final moments of the play, when the music emerges for the last time. As with the end of Act II, the room is shot here from the position general view at A, and once again the music is audible from this point. Now, however, it swells and plays right to the end. What is more, Beckett is explicit at III.37 that its source cannot be seen: 'close-up of head bowed right down over cassette now held in arms and invisible'. The music, in other words, is completely non-diegetic and allowed to unfold to full effect.

This final scene is dominated by a close-up that echoes, but does not repeat, the face in the mirror of III.27. That is to say, whereas the rest of the Act is structured through a return to key actions from Act II seen from new angles, it ends with an inexact, but overt, imitation of a previous action in Act III.

The nature of the temporality of the play also changes at this moment. So far, Act III has faithfully repeated Act II, but rather than simply repeating the end, Act III extends it, continuing for another several minutes. This results in what seems to be another, final challenge to V, and her injunction at the end of Act II to 'Repeat', for although the rest of F's basic actions echo the events of the previous Act, the final moments are new, and V's voice is absent. Here is the end of Act II:

II.35. *Faint music audible for first time at A. It grows louder. 5 seconds.*
   II.36. V. Stop.
   II.37. *Music stops. General view from A. 5 seconds.*
   II.38. V. Repeat.

And this is the end of Act III.
      III.36. *Music audible at A. It grows. 10 seconds.*
      III.37. *With growing music move in slowly to close-up of head bowed right down over cassette now held in arms and invisible. Hold till end of Largo.*
      III.38. *Silence. F raises head. Face seen clearly for second time. 10 seconds.*
      III.39. *Move slowly back to A.*
      III.40. *General view from A. 5 seconds.*
      III.41. *Fade out.*

Both sequences feature the music's encroachment on the position general view. Where V stops the music at II.37 after five seconds, however, III.36 extends the Beethoven fragment and allows it to continue for ten. At the same time, the camera begins to penetrate into the scene in a manner familiar from previous movements of approach to and withdrawal from to F's seated figure. As in the exploratory sequence ending in the image of F's face in the mirror, a balance is struck between our absorption into the world of the play and a theatrical address to us. Now that the music is allowed to unfold to its conclusion, we feel its full emotional and affective force. Yet because the camera is held until the Largo finishes and only then moves out again, there is no opportunity to have the music fade with increasing distance from F. In this way the naturalism of the sequence's use of music is subtly qualified.

The bowed head, a central motif for Beckett throughout his work, explicitly harks back to III.27: 'Head bows. Top of head in mirror'. It is an image of absorption of the most explicit kind, and the music powerfully influences our gaze upon it. It as if the resistance of F has finally been overcome. But Beckett now states in III.37 that the source of the music, the recorder, must be concealed, making the question of the relationship between sound and image part of the mystery of the scene. This shot, the last appearance of music in the play, also speaks back to the Largo's very first, when its faint sounds accompanied the image of the door. In each case sound and image are both superimposed upon and detached from each other.

When the music stops, Beckett reverses the action in III.27, where F's face was gradually occluded as he bowed his head. Now, in the silence after the last notes of the Largo, F slowly lifts his head to gaze at the camera directly for ten seconds (Figure 11). As Beckett makes clear in the stage directions, this is a moment that is intended to recall the previous image of F's face. But there is no doubling of the image in the mirror here, and no closing of the eyes. The irony and ambiguity of object and reflection that had hedged around the previous shot of the face is dispensed with. What we are left with is, for the first time, a direct address from F to the audience, an explicit acknowledgement of the beholder located at the position general view. And yet it is important to remember that this moment, which extends the action of Act II, also escapes it. V had ended Act II with the injunction 'Repeat', but this is not a repetition of anything that happened there: it is entirely new. The intriguing question that arises, then, is whether F is still acting or not. In the absence of V's voice, and after the end of the music that, to some extent, substituted for it, perhaps it is the case that this acknowledgement of the beholder takes place outside the parameters of the play. Put differently, the actor is addressing the audience in a way he is disallowed from doing in the course of the play; he has definitively stepped out of character and is effectively taking a bow. If this is correct, then the play actually ends at the same place it does in Act II, with F's bowed head, and the rest is a curtain call. What had seemed to be a resolution of the opposition between barring and direct address is thrown into doubt.

Figure 11 Beckett, *Ghost Trio*, BBC, 1977

11 Conclusion

Ghost Trio directs and manipulates the gaze of its beholder in ways that Michael Fried would term theatrical. It acknowledges the gaze of the viewer; indeed, it goes much further than this, attempting to snare the eye, working, in Fried's precise and apposite term, to *neutralise* the beholder (Fried, 1988, 68). Hence, 'Dust', says the Voice that accompanies the abstract, framed images that flash up on the screen throughout Act I. And yet we do not see the dust. All we see is a dark grey rectangle on a lighter one, or a light grey rectangle on a darkened one. 'Look again', says the Voice, as if our eye, having been made aware of the texture of the real through the close-up, will now see the scene properly and so body it forth in all its ontological density. But we do not, no matter how the voice invites and importunes us. In Act I, V's speech attempts, in what seems from the vantage of Act III to be a pre-emptive move, to school the viewer in the appropriate attitude towards objects, sponsoring a cognitive attitude where the part can stand for the whole, and objects can be effortlessly brought under concepts. Despite V's confident theatrical address, however, the viewer's grasp of the close-ups partakes not of a cognitive judgement but rather something more like an aesthetic one. The shapes of the specimen of floor and wall in particular seem calculated to excite a play of the faculties rather than a substantive or definitive conclusion of the kind implied by V.

In Act II other devices are employed, despite the objectivity of V as affectless guide, and the suspension of acting in favour of Cavellian happening. In Act III, meanwhile, there is a carefully patterned structure of point-of-view shots whereby we effectively *become* F. Nevertheless, Beckett is also always working to ensure that a certain resistance ensues: 'To restore silence is the role of objects', he famously writes in *Molloy*, and *Ghost Trio*'s objects – mirror, cassette, pallet – are the late epitome of this dictum (Beckett, 1979, 12). Indeed, F himself becomes an object at the crucial point when he mimics his own death mask, and V's gasp before it is more evidence of the errancy, the inadequacy, of her attempt to attune the audience to this singular image-world. And it is in this spirit too that the close-ups of Act III hark back to the rectangles of Act I. To take one final example of the play's various stratagems, at times it is music that seems to enable us to get the measure of the room, as the eye is guided through the introduction of the Beethoven score. Yet this too is a ruse, as is eventually emphasized by the very end of the drama.

Ghost Trio's laying bare of the conventions of theatricality and absorption emphasizes what Michael Fried terms the 'to-be-seenness' of the play, its formal preoccupation with the relation of artwork to beholder at a moment of crisis. At the same time, the play is also cognizant of a variety of other issues around the question of beholding that turn on the question of the ontological difference of the respective worlds that image and beholder occupy. Over the course of its three Acts, the world of *Ghost Trio* systematically detaches itself from, and then returns to, the world of the beholder. 'His landscape is as if there are no eyes left in the world', said Beckett of one of Karl Kluth's pictures, and *Ghost Trio* too partakes at times of a similar impossible objecthood (Carville, 2018, 104–5).

With all this in mind, I want to end with another quotation from Cavell, on modernist painting of the 1960s:

> These are works every one of whose properties is essential to them. This is the definition of a Leibnizian monad. Like a monad, like the world there is, the only fact about these paintings that does not follow analytically from a complete idea of them is that they exist in space and time. Existence in this world, like the existence of the world itself, is the only contingent fact about them. They are themselves, I feel like saying, contingencies, realizations. (Cavell, 1979b, 116)

The notion of the artwork as monad is a common modernist idea, found in Adorno, Benjamin and Auden as well as Beckett. The monad is Leibniz's strange, famously sealed, 'windowless' unit, which both contains all other monads and is itself an autonomous entity. For Beckett it is associated with the desire to access the in-itself, the realm beyond the correlation between the human subject and object (Carville, 2018, 106–8). The monad is a token of an inhuman materiality, graspable only when the human is erased. As such, Beckett associates it with death and a range of metaphors of petrification, minerality, dust and the inorganic.

In Cavell and Fried the sense of the monad is less extreme, more humanistic, and can be understood as another iteration of the autonomous modernist artwork, the poem or painting whose intricately self-referential material form subtracts it from the world, suspends it, so that it functions through the pure play of its own matrices, becoming a world itself. Our acknowledgement of this powerful autonomy is the primary role of the reader or beholder. The audience does not complete the artwork by apprehending it, in the empirical way that V enjoins us to grasp the rectangles of Act I. Quite the contrary: the audience is struck first by, and must grant, the artwork's imperturbable, disinterested detachment. Cavell in particular goes on to draw ethical lessons from this for respect and recognition in the social world. Beckett, however, is more drawn to the metaphysical. Acknowledgement of the monadic artwork is not parlayed into acceptance of the otherness of the human other, but rather entails a rare insight into the primordially inhuman nature of the void over which the human skates. It is here that Beckett's essentially Schopenhauerean pessimism, his vision of 'the indestructible chaos of timeless things', prevails over any Kantian sense of purposiveness guaranteeing the cognizing of nature or the pleasures of beauty (Beckett, 1979, 38). Having said that, as I hope I have shown, Cavell and Fried's foregrounding of ideas of character, the beholder/audience and the nature of the visual artwork provide a very useful framework for getting at what is actually going on in *Ghost Trio*. The key assumption that joins Beckett, Cavell and Fried is that the successful work of art stages an ontology of separation, a denial of the audience (Cavell) or beholder (Fried) that speaks to, reveals, a more general separation, which Cavell calls scepticism, and Beckett the 'issueless predicament of existence'. The latter phrase, taken from Beckett's valediction to Jack B. Yeats, refers to the dearth of exit or exchange as the *sine qua non* of Beckett's grim ontology.

For Cavell, such issuelessness is staged by the destruction of the 'concept and status of the audience' that accompanies Beckett's abandonment of character and acting, his reduction of drama to sheer happening, to occurring: 'Something is taking its course', says Clov, though he has no insight into what that thing is. And crucially, nor does the audience (Cavell often parallels the relationship between performer and performer as sceptical, and then sees this as mirroring the relationship between play and audience. Beckett does the same with painting). The thing that takes its course is indiscernable, like the thing that unites God, man and protoplast in Beckett's essay 'The New Object (Beckett, 2011, 880). Or 'the invisible thing' that painting must address, as Beckett puts it in 'Le Monde et le Pantalon' (Beckett, 1983, 130). By finding a replacement for candidness (or absorption) in the 'thing' that is 'happening', Beckett absolutizes the border between actor and audience. He makes the invisible thing available 'not in the head' of the audience, but on the stage. (In Brecht, by contrast, the appeal to complicity means the border is erased, the actors appeal directly to the audience.) As Cavell puts it, for such a theatre God is the only audience, the gaze *sub specie aeternitatis* (Cavell, 1976a, 154). And this is how Beckett sees the painting he admires: the only beholder it is addressed to is an impossible one, a pure objectivity, a single monad that contains the universe.

Beckett's life-long attraction to inorganic, inhuman figures sits comfortably within this constellation of ideas. Cavell finds something similar in Shakespeare, bringing actor and character together through the concept of the marionette: 'Othello is not pretending. Garrick is not pretending, any more than a puppet in that part would be pretending' (Cavell, 1976b, 330). And when he is summing up his understanding of Beckett's work he reaches for the fourth of Rilke's *Duino Elegies*, where the vision of man as marionette finds one of its most exquisite modernist articulations. Cavell:

Solitude, emptiness, nothingness, meaninglessness, silence, these are not the givens of Beckett's characters but their goal, their new heroic undertaking. To say that Beckett's message is that the world is meaningless, etc. is as ironically and dead wrong as to say it of Kierkegaard or Nietzsche or Rilke, for whom emptiness or perfect singleness are not states – not here and now – but infinite tasks. Achieving them will require passing the edge of madness, maybe passing over, and certainly passing through horror, bearing the nausea Zarathustra knows or the vision of oneself as a puppet ('the husk, the wire, even the face that's all outside') as in Rilke's fourth Duino Elegy – not protesting one's emptiness, but seeing what one is filled with. Then the angel may appear, then nature, then things, then others, then, if ever, the fullness of time; then, if ever, the achievement of the ordinary, the faith to be plain, or not to be. (Cavell, 1976a, 156)

'Perfect singleness as a task', 'not protesting one's emptiness, but seeing what one is filled with'. These descriptions are exactly right and express the monadic kenosis that Cavell finds enacted in both Beckett and Shakespeare. For Cavell and Fried, such emptying out issues in the fullness of 'grace'. It is such 'instantaneousness' that for Beckett distinguishes the work of van Velde, Yeats and Cezanne. In all cases it is through an operation on the beholder or audience *as* precisely beholder or audience that the fullness of time, happening, *kairos* occurs. This is the suspension of performance, of empathic projection, that Fried terms 'to-be-seenness'.

When Beckett says to Ruby Cohn, 'the figure resisted me, so I resorted to rectangles', he allies the sensuous plenitude of the inner storm with the austere abstraction of Act I's close-ups of 'dust', and we get a glimpse of his aesthetic thinking, usually exercised in his comments on painting, applied to his own work. For Beckett, the dream of a pure access to interiority is cognate with the severe abstraction of the rectangle. In the end it is the recognition of the material resistance, the impenetrability of the absorbed other, that provides the passage through scepticism. This resistance itself is staged, figured, in the constant, flickering formal movement between the general and the particular, mimesis and abstraction, convention and the failure of convention, character and happening. In the process the author and viewer gain access to, as Beckett put it of Yeat's 'The Storm', their own singularity. Beckett once admiringly described the characteristic painting by Yeats as a 'man alone thinking (thinking!) in his box' (Beckett, 1983, 97). This relationship between the thought of the other and the form in which it is presented to an audience is also the resistant, dusty, compacted kernel of *Ghost Trio*.

References

Bazin, André (1967), *What is Cinema? Vol. 1*, Berkeley: University of California Press.

Beckett, Samuel (1936–7), *German Diaries*, UoR MS, Beckett International Foundation, University of Reading.

Beckett, Samuel (1965), *Proust and Three Dialogues*, London: Calder.

Beckett, Samuel (1976a), *Ghost Trio*, UoR MS1519/1, Beckett International Foundation, University of Reading.

Beckett, Samuel (1976b), 'Notes on Tryst', UoR 1519/3, Beckett International Foundation, University of Reading.

Beckett, Samuel (1979), *The Beckett Trilogy: Molloy, Malone Dies, The Unnamable*, London: Picador.

Beckett, Samuel (1983), *Disjecta; Miscellaneous Writings and a Dramatic Fragment*, ed. Ruby Cohn, London: Calder.

Beckett, Samuel (1989), 'First Love', in *The Expelled and Other Novellas*, London: Penguin.

Beckett, Samuel (1990), *The Complete Dramatic Works*, London: Faber and Faber.

Beckett, Samuel (2009), *The Letters of Samuel Beckett, Vol. 1: 1929–1940*, ed. Martha Fehsenfeld and Lois More Overbeck, Cambridge: Cambridge University Press.

Beckett, Samuel (2010), *Texts for Nothing and Other Shorter Prose, 1950–1976*, ed. Mark Nixon, London: Faber and Faber.

Beckett, Samuel (2011), 'The New Object', *Modernism/modernity*, 18:4, pp. 878–80.

Caillois, Roger (2003), 'Mimicry and Legendary Psychasthenia', in Claudine Frank (ed.), *The Edge of Surrealism: A Roger Caillois Reader*, Durham, NC: Duke University Press, pp. 89–107.

Carville, Conor (2018), *Samuel Beckett and the Visual Arts*, Cambridge: Cambridge University Press.

Cavell, Stanley (1976a), 'Ending the Waiting Game: A Reading of Beckett's *Endgame*', in *Must We Mean What We Say*, Cambridge: Cambridge University Press, pp. 115–62.

Cavell, Stanley (1976b), 'The Avoidance of Love: A Reading of *King Lear*', in *Must We Mean What We Say*, Cambridge: Cambridge University Press, pp. 267–356.

Cavell, Stanley (1979a), *The Claim of Reason: Wittgenstein, Scepticism, Morality and Tragedy*, Oxford: Oxford University Press.

Cavell, Stanley (1979b), *The World Viewed: Reflections on the Ontology of Film*, Cambridge, MA: Harvard University Press.

Cohn, Ruby (2005), *A Beckett Canon*, Ann Arbor: University of Michigan Press.

Fried, Michael (1988), *Absorption and Theatricality: Painting and Beholder in the Age of Diderot*, Chicago, IL: University of Chicago Press.

Fried, Michael (1992), *Courbet's Realism*, Chicago, IL: University of Chicago Press.

Fried, Michael (1998), *Art and Objecthood: Essays and Reviews*, Chicago, IL: University of Chicago Press.

Fried, Michael (1999), *Manet's Modernism: Or, The Face of Painting in the 1860s*, Chicago, IL: University of Chicago Press.

Fried, Michael (2008), *Why Photography Matters as Art as Never Before*, New Haven, CT, and London: Yale University Press.

Fried, Michael (2011), *Four Honest Outlaws: Marioni, Ray, Sala, Gordon*, New Haven, CT, and London: Yale University Press.

Greenberg, Clement (2002), 'Modernist Painting', in Charles Harrison and Paul Wood (eds.), *Art in Theory 1900–2000: An Anthology of Changing Ideas*, Oxford: Blackwell, pp. 773–9.

Herren, Graley (2007), *Samuel Beckett's Plays on Film and TV*, New York: Palgrave.

Kleist, Heinrich von (1982), 'On the Puppet Theatre', in Philip B. Miller (trans., ed., and introduction), *An Abyss Deep Enough: Letters of Heinrich von Kleist with a Selection of Essays and Anecdotes*, New York: Dutton, pp. 211–16.

Knowlson, James (2009), 'Beckett and Seventeenth-Century Dutch and Flemish Art', *Beckett Today / Aujourd'hui*, 21, pp. 27–44.

Knowlson, James, and John Pilling (1979), *Frescoes of the Skull: The Later Prose and Drama of Samuel Beckett*, London: Calder.

Cambridge Elements ⹀

Beckett Studies

Dirk Van Hulle
University of Oxford

Dirk Van Hulle is Professor of Bibliography and Modern Book History at the University of Oxford and director of the Centre for Manuscript Genetics at the University of Antwerp.

Mark Nixon
University of Reading

Mark Nixon is Associate Professor in Modern Literature at the University of Reading and the Co-director of the Beckett International Foundation.

About the Series

This series presents cutting-edge research by distinguished and emerging scholars, providing space for the most relevant debates informing Beckett studies as well as neglected aspects of his work. In times of technological development, religious radicalism, unprecedented migration, gender fluidity, environmental and social crisis, Beckett's works find increased resonance. Cambridge Elements in Beckett Studies is a key resource for readers interested in the current state of the field.